A Better Life

A Better Life

MICHAEL JENET

Guide Point North Publishing
Colorado, U.S.A.

Guide Point North Publishing
An imprint of Journey Institute Press,
a division of 50 in 52 Journey, Inc.
journeyinstitutepress.org

Copyright © 2025 Michael Jenet
All rights reserved.

Journey Institute Press supports copyright. Copyright allows artistic creativity, encourages diverse voices, and promotes free speech. Thank you for purchasing an authorized edition of this work and for complying with copyright laws by not reproducing, scanning, or distributing any part of this work in any form without permission.

Library of Congress Control Number: 2025947152
Names: Jenet, Michael
Title: A Better Life
Description: Colorado: Guide Poiont North Publishing, 2025

Identifiers: ISBN 978-1-964754-43-7 (hardcover)
ISBN 978-1-964754-44-4 (paperback)
ISBN 978-1-964754-45-1 (ebook/kindle)

Subjects: BISAC:
SELF-HELP / Personal Growth / Success |
SELF-HELP / Dreams |
BODY, MIND,& SPIRIT / Inspirational & Personal Growth |

Second Edition
Printed in the United States of America

2 3 7 11 16 39 40 47 50 81

This book was typeset in EB Garamond / Dancing Script
Editing by Jessica Medberry, InkWhale Editorial LLC.
Cover design by WiggleB Studios

For Dafna,
My muse in all things.

Chapter 1
Boxing With Life

I knew if my head hit the ground; it was all over.

I had been looking up at the sky, at the vastness of the universe with all its stars and wonderment and mystery. After a while, my gaze dropped to the horizon, and I stared at the thin line where earth and sky meet. I watched the cloud formations and various colors that paint the canvas each time the sun trades places with the moon. Soon I found myself comfortably appreciating those sunrises and sunsets as they reflected off the waves of the ocean.

Before long, I found my eyes following the waves as they lapped onto the shore, their soothing sounds and overturning whitecaps fizzing as the water crested on the beach before slowly ebbing back into the great "deep blue." Dropping my gaze further still, I watched as the water caresses my toes. I could feel the comfort of the soft sand as it spread with the oncoming water, before sucking at my feet as the waves retreated to the ocean.

I'm content, comfortable, breathing deeply with a gentle sigh. Then a voice disrupts my thoughts. "Hey."

At first I look behind me, unsure of where the sound is coming from, but no one is there. I slowly turn my head forward and notice that he is standing right in front of me.

It's Life.

He doesn't look at all pleased.

I frown, confused, unsure of what I have done to upset him. There is little time to ponder the thought, though I never sense the danger. I never see it coming. It is only at the last moment that my instincts kick in and I react.

Life's right hand is moving at an alarming speed, and it heads straight for my face. More specifically, it is the bright red of his boxing glove that flashes through my mind's eye milliseconds before he connects.

The blow is jarring. Blood pours from my nostrils as the dull roar of pain begins to ring in my ears and spread through my nervous system. I stagger a few steps backward from the impact. I have no time for questions. Life is advancing, and his left hook is already on its way.

I put my arms up now, more instinct than a structured defense. I block his hook with my right forearm, though the weight of his punch is frightening. I can already begin to feel my arm going numb. Both my hands are up now, in front of my face, fists bunched as though I might know what I am doing. Truth be told, my brain is just mimicking what I have seen in the movies. Still, I am able to block two more punches, each one adding bruises to the ones from before as my forearms begin to swell.

There is no time to process, no time for thought. Life's assault is relentless and lightning fast. Just as I block another left jab, he swings his right in a loop and with a much lower trajectory. His body pivots as he puts his shoulder behind the punch. It lands thunderously into my left side, cracking a few ribs with a sickening sound. It knocks the wind out of my lungs and sends me careening backward off the beach and onto the hardened dirt path beyond.

The pain is beyond anything I have felt before. I begin to panic, gasping for air as I watch LIFE continue his advance. I get my arms back up to defend my head as he begins a barrage of jabs, uppercuts, and looping side punches. Although I get a hand up to block one or two, the force of his blows slams my arm humiliatingly against my head, sending bell-like cacophonies ringing throughout my mind and knocking me further and further backward, step after step from punch after punch.

What little air I take in is expelled in a rush as an uppercut plunges deep into my stomach, lifting me a few inches off the ground and landing me jarringly back before I take several steps in retreat. I'm stumbling, twisting, and scrambling in an effort to get away from this monstrous attack. My body is now bent over in pain; my eyes open to see the cold, hard ground beneath me. Fear seizes my heart in renewed panic and spreads faster than light through my bloodstream. Ice-cold sweat breaks out on my forehead as alarms go off in every nerve center of my being. I can . . . not . . . fall. *I must not fall down!*

LIFE senses my fear and springs forward with shocking agility. The barrage comes faster and harder than before, and there is no way for me to defend myself. The bruises and broken bones mount as LIFE lands blow after deafening blow. My limbs are no longer able to protect me, as my mind is too numb to react and form even the meekest of defenses.

In a moment that appears as if in slow motion, just like in those movies, I watch helplessly as LIFE's entire body moves in harmony behind his last punch. His muscles ripple with power, legs slightly apart as he leads with his right foot, his right hand following over it. I watch as the shoulder muscles bunch with menacing fluidity and the red bulbous head of the boxing glove moves toward me, inch by terrifying inch. Holding his breath until the punch lands, then expelling it in a loud whooshing sound that echoes inside my mind just before the force of the blow registers, he smashes the glove into the side of my head.

The blow is crushing. With no protection, no last-second turn in defense, no strength left at all, I crumble. I sense more than feel my head snap to the side as I expel blood and saliva from my mouth like a rush of water from a hose. My nervous system, jarred by this final strike, momentarily short-circuits, and my body caves in on itself, giving in to gravity as I inevitably fall face forward to the ground.

Surprisingly, my mind flashes with a speed I would not have thought possible given my current state. The flashes, however, are not comforting.

Knowing that I am falling, that all is lost, that everything I had as that person standing on the beach with the water flowing over my toes—it's going forever. I'm losing it all. Only the cold, hard, and unforgiving ground is waiting as I fall closer and closer to it. I know the pain of the impact will be immeasurable, yet my mind races, not with fear, but with sadness at all that I have lost. Sure, fear raises its voice in momentary protests at what will happen when my body hits the ground, yet it is the overwhelming sense of loss that grips me.

Beyond the point of no return now, my body in the final few feet of gravity's pull, one last flash of desperation leaves my cerebral cortex and spurs on the last vestiges of energy in the nerves throughout my beaten body. In one coordinated series of agonizing muscle-controlling pulses, the nerves frantically command my body to turn. At the very last possible moment, I somehow drop my shoulder, half turning my upper torso.

The impact as my shoulder hits the rock-hard earth is almost too much to bear, but the momentum of my body's final act does the trick. Rather than landing face first, the side of my head hits the ground and I flop onto my back. My arms splay out to my sides, and my legs go limp as they slide out flat before me. None of this registers with any actual thought, as the blow from the side of my head hitting the ground renders me unconscious.

When I wake up, the first sensation is pain.

Unimaginable pain. Pain in every part of my being. Stabbing, relentless shards of agony in my sides, in my head, in my lungs, in every muscle and fiber of my body.

Where the stabbing is absent, there is throbbing, aching pain, and if any other part of me is not aching, it is engulfed in spasms as my muscles and nerves protest with sharp electric pulses, each more painful than the last.

I slowly open my eyes, trying to focus. Am I dead? Is death supposed to be this painful? The thoughts are not coherent, just more flashes of impulses in my mind. Somehow, I lift my head just enough to look down before me, and there, standing at my feet, is LIFE.

The boxing gloves are no longer on his hands. The look on his face is no longer one of anger, nor is it one of triumph or pleasure. His feet shoulder-width apart and his bare hands on his hips, he looks down at me, tilting his head from side to side. His brow furrowed. The look on his face is a mixture of anxiety, concern, and curiosity.

I let my head fall slowly back to the hard, cold ground beneath me. My eyes go in and out of focus for a moment. As the blurriness clears, my brain reorganizes itself, and it hits me.

Multiple thoughts flash across my mind.

I realize that when I was standing at the water's edge on the beach and looking up at the stars and the sky, I was dreaming. The kind of dreams I dreamt as a child.

My mind had been completely open to limitless possibilities, and the vastness of the universe was alive with all that I was capable of doing. But then time went by, and I had dropped my gaze from the stars to the horizon. I had wondered what lay beyond it. My mind still curious and receptive, I had marveled at the thoughts of what it would be like to explore and discover.

Still, eventually, I'd begun gazing at the sunrise and sunset, at their beauty and consistency, until even gazing off into the distance lost its appeal and I focused instead on the waves.

I became comfortable with the sand over my feet. The ebb and flow of the waves against the shore. No longer concerned with my dreams in the sky or the adventures of the horizon, I had stared down at my place on the beach, comforted by the warmth of the water and the slow and steady erosion of the sand against my skin.

This realization flashes before my mind, followed by three more glaring thoughts.

The first is that I am still alive. Despite LIFE's beating; despite the painful assault and ultimate failure to keep standing, to hold on to what I had; despite the crushing fall and jarring landing on the cold, hard ground—I am still breathing.

The second thought is that now that I have fallen and I am lying on the ground, there is nowhere to go but up!

Which then leads to the third and final thought. The most amazing of them all.

As I lie on the ground and my eyes come back into focus, I realize I am, once again, looking up at the stars!

Chapter 2
Waking Up

I woke up stiff and aching all over.

I opened my eyes slowly, afraid of what I would see. I was in my house, in my favorite chair in the attic-cum-den, to be precise. It was one of those soft brown leather chairs that reclines, with overstuffed arms and big claw feet. I looked around the room at the shelves on the walls to either side, stuffed with all my favorite books, and the piles, here and there, of books I still had yet to read.

There in the corner was a bright green fern. It sat on a wrought-iron table with patterned tile, which Mary had found in the antique shop. Why she kept buying ferns when I kept killing them was a mystery, but I had to admit I loved the color of green against the dark brown of the wood that made up most of my sanctuary. Well, not a sanctuary, per se; I enjoyed being married to Mary and spending time with her, but this was my room. Full of my books, my computer, my desk. The one room in the house I could retreat to if I needed to think or wanted to read without hearing a phone conversation or the neighbor dropping by. It was also a great place to hide when Mary was traveling for her work.

I must have fallen asleep in the chair. I was stiff, and my neck had a crick in it from the way I had been lying, half in and half out of the chair.

That dream—it must have been a dream. *Obviously it was a dream,* I thought, shaking my head at the memory of my fight with LIFE. That wasn't a good idea, as the shaking resulted in a pounding headache.

It had been so vivid, so real. I gazed out the tall window at the end of the room. The den, more an attic converted into a makeshift office, was just big enough to hold the bookshelves, the dark mahogany desk I inherited from my father when he passed away, and the low round coffee table that was in front of my chair. It all suited me well. The window, tall for a gable window, gave me a beautiful view of our neighborhood and the city beyond, and on a clear night like tonight, an unobstructed view of Colorado's Rocky Mountains with the sky above them.

The sky. The stars. The dream had been so vivid. I sat and stared out the window at the cloudless sky. It was like a black drape had been thrown over the planet, with small holes poked in it where the stars' light shone through. We lived far enough away from the city to see stars now and again, though the light from Denver often made it difficult.

I pushed myself up in the chair, letting the leg rest retract beneath it as I tried to work the kinks out of my body. I was sore all right, though nothing near the pummeling I had dreamed about. My mind must have connected the view out of the window with my body's aches and pains from falling asleep in the chair and let my subconscious run wild. Surely that explained everything.

I turned off the mica shade lamp on my desk and headed for the door. As I was about to close it behind me, I looked one more time out of the window at the sky and the blanket of twinkling stars. When was the last time I had thought about my goals and dreams? Did I even know what they were anymore?

Marlow, our golden retriever, came bounding up the stairs, interrupting my thoughts. He often came into the den when I was there, but he had been eating his dinner when I went up earlier that night. I ruffled his golden-brown fur, receiving a slobbery lick on my hand in return.

Mary was in bed doing something on her iPad when I walked in. She was propped up on our king-sized bed with six pillows behind her. It always made me laugh that she needed so many pillows on her side of the bed when I only needed one.

She looked up as Marlow and I came through the door. "There you are," she said, smiling. "I was about to come and find you."

"Yeah." I smiled. "Sorry, I fell asleep in my chair."

Mary frowned a little. "Are you OK? You've been doing that more often lately." Then she added, "And you have not been sleeping through the night much either." Her last remark had that mothering tone in it.

"Yes, I'm fine," I said, not wanting to discuss the stress I was feeling at work because I knew it would just worry her.

As I changed into my pajamas, she said with a heavy sigh, "Well, tomorrow we say goodbye to Doug and Alison."

Doug and Alison Wallberg were some of our closest friends. We had met them soon after we moved to Colorado. Alison and Mary had hit it off, and Doug and I, by proxy, had turned out to be quite good friends as well. Even though they lived about as far away on the other side of Denver as possible, we still saw each other a couple of times a month. Mary talked to Alison on the phone almost every day, and Doug and I would catch up either by email or on weekends when we'd help each other with various projects.

All that was going to change now. Doug was in insurance and Alison had run an antique shop, which was where Mary had bought the stand for the plant in the den. Going to sub-Saharan Africa had long been on both of their "bucket lists." So, with little warning but the time it took for them to sell their house, Alison had also sold her business, and Doug had turned in his notice. They were leaving tomorrow, with little in the way of an actual plan, as far as I could see, but with a great deal of guts and determination to follow their dreams and move to Africa. I hadn't seen either of them as excited about anything for a long time as they were about their adventure.

A light bulb went off in my head, and I realized it was probably Doug and Alison's impending departure to follow their dreams that had played a role in my boxing-match dream earlier. It all made sense. I was upset at losing some of our best friends as they were gearing up to go halfway across the world. Combined with the clear star-filled sky tonight and my uncomfortable contortion in my armchair, no wonder I'd had such an odd dream.

"Don't forget," Mary said, "we need to pick them up by eight thirty to get them to the airport on time, and with rush hour we'll need to leave a little earlier than normal."

I nodded as I climbed under the deep burgundy down comforter we had on the bed for the cold Colorado nights we had been having this winter. I thought about telling Mary about my dream, but what was the point? After all, I had just found the explanation for it, and if I told her, she might think it had something to do with my not sleeping at night or the stress at work. That was something I was not going to touch with a ten-foot pole if I could help it.

Mary packed in her iPad, leaned over to give me a kiss, and then turned off her bedside light. I lay in the dark for a while, listening to her drifting off to sleep. The soft sound of her breathing slowed to a gentle rhythm as she lay on her side facing me. She murmured that she loved me in her half-asleep state and rolled over. Her sleep was fitful and I envied her, though I knew she would be awake before me, reading blogs and news from her phone sometime around five o'clock, or if she was really tired, six.

I would fall asleep for an hour or two and then be awake for two or three more before falling back asleep just as Mary was close to waking. It was a pattern that had started almost eight months ago. I knew it was stress from work, but there was little I could do about that.

I tried to think of something to occupy my mind, but no matter what I thought about, I kept replaying the dream in my head. Try as I might to explain it away, my mind kept focusing on it. My dreams and goals. Where had they gone? Did I even know what they were now or what they once had been? I fell asleep eventually, but not before I saw Life's face screwed up with rage as his red-gloved fist came hurtling toward my head.

We picked Doug and Alison up with five minutes to spare, despite an accident on I-25 and heavier-than-usual traffic for a Wednesday. This, of course, was all thanks to Mary's brilliant use of the GPS on her phone. It took us via a circuitous route through parts of the Denver Metro area I didn't even know existed, and it helped us move around the congestion.

With the suitcases packed in the car, we were on our way. We were heading south to go northeast, but Mary assured me, based on her GPS, that this would get us there faster than the straighter shot on the highway.

I didn't argue. An information technology career I might have, but when it came to apps on mobile devices, no one was more adept than Mary.

The girls were in the back, chatting happily; Alison giggled and laughed with glee at the plans she and Doug had already made for the first month after they arrived in Africa. Doug had already regaled me with much of it a few weeks ago, when I'd helped him move the rest of the belongings they had not given away or sold into long-term storage.

As I navigated my way through the morning traffic, Doug looked over and said in a voice low enough that our wives wouldn't be able to hear, "You don't look like things are any better than they were a month ago, my friend."

I had hoped he would forget that conversation. We had been packing up boxes at Alison's Fine Antiques, and somehow I had talked about work and how stressful things were. Doug had been alarmed when I told him about my not sleeping and some things I was dealing with at the office.

"That doesn't sound like much of a fun place to work," he had said. Then, "You can't keep going on like this, buddy."

We ended up talking for hours, sitting in the back room over the worn barn wood table Alison had used to pack and unpack the boxes of items moving through her store. The more we talked, the more concerned Doug had become. He tried to help me figure out a way to leave my job, to find another one with less stress, but the truth was, I was stuck. I was finally at the top of my career, making decent money, and while Mary made a good salary, it was half of what I made. We didn't live extravagant lives by any stretch of the imagination, but I could not afford a pay cut, and that is what would happen if I switched jobs.

I had said as much to Doug that night over pizza, but he had been relentless. One thing I loved about him was his passion, and he had been fired up that night, pacing back and forth while coming up with one wild scenario after another about how to help me get away from what he referred to as "the job that is eating your soul."

Since then, Doug had been swamped with getting things ready for the trip. I had hoped he had forgotten that night or at least had given up, but it seemed I was mistaken.

I glanced over at him. "I'm fine," I said, knowing full well he knew I was lying.

"Right," he replied with a big grin on his face. "And I'm Goldilocks."

Alison heard that one and piped up from the back of the car, "What? Why are you Goldilocks, babe?"

Doug half turned in his seat and said, "Nothing, hon, just a joke." Then he added, "Did you tell Mary about that last email from the river tour guide?"

That set Alison off on another squeal-filled story as she and Mary inched closer in the back seat like high school girls on a double date sharing secrets.

Doug turned back to face the front and then looked over at me. He said nothing for a few minutes. When he spoke, his voice was low and even—calm, yet somehow commanding. "You know you can't keep this up much longer. Have you thought at all about what you're going to do?"

I made an exaggerated show of looking at all my car mirrors as I turned left across one of southeast Denver's busiest major thoroughfares, trying to think of an answer that would pacify my friend. I knew he meant well, but this wasn't a conversation I wanted to have.

Finally, with a heavy sigh, I said, "It's not that simple, Doug. I told you, if I look and find something, which is doubtful"—I said this somewhat pointedly as I glanced over at him—"there's no way I'd make as much, and I would just be starting all over again. I just can't afford to do that."

Doug never missed a beat, as though he had expected my answer, and said, "I know it seems like that to you, and I am not saying that what you feel isn't real to you, but listen to me when I tell you, pal, you cannot afford not to do something."

Thankfully, we were approaching the airport. The usual cluster of cars were jockeying for position as they approached the drop-off area for their respective airlines. I found an opening in front of Lufthansa and snuck in before someone else took it.

We all piled out, and Doug and I began unloading the suitcases as Alison and Mary began crying and hugging each other. With all the bags on the sidewalk, I gave Alison a hug, trying desperately not to cry myself. Alison was one of those people who gives strong, long-lasting hugs. The kind where you feel as though she is trying to remember every part of how you feel as she wraps her arms around you, holding you as close as she can and squeezing you as hard as her tiny frame allows.

I loved Alison's hugs, and by the time she let me go, I had lost the battle with my tear ducts.

I wiped the tears away as Doug and I exchanged a big bear hug.

"Let us know when you get there, OK?" I said, blinking furiously.

He, too, was taking deep breaths. "Yeah, absolutely." Then, reaching into his coat, he said, "Listen, I want you to do me one last favor."

"Sure," I replied, "what do you need?"

"I want you to meet a friend of mine two weeks from now." He pulled out a plain white envelope from his pocket and handed it to me.

I took it. It was sealed, with no writing on the outside. It looked like it had a small card inside. "Sure," I said hesitantly. "What's this all about?"

Doug turned and started stacking suitcases onto the cart Alison had bought from a nearby stand. "It's just a lunch meeting. Do it for me, OK?"

"Uhhh . . . sure," I said, putting the envelope in my coat pocket, still confused about why he wanted me to have a lunch meeting. "Are you going to tell me anything about who this person is?"

"It's all in there," he said, motioning to the envelope. Then, putting the last bag on the now teetering pile of suitcases atop the cart, he said, "OK, I think that's everything. Hopefully, the weight limit on the plane is over two tons." That garnered a "Hey" from Alison and a rebuke of "Doug, you know a girl needs her shoes in the jungle" from Mary.

We all laughed, and just like that, Mary and I were waving as Doug and Alison took their cart in through the sliding doors and disappeared among the throng of other passengers entering the airport.

We got back in the car just as a traffic cop was headed our way to tell us to move, and I edged back into the centipede-like file of cars snaking its way out of the airport.

I took out Doug's envelope as we headed down Peña Boulevard, and holding it against the steering wheel with one hand, I opened it with the other. Inside was a small white card, only slightly bigger than a business card, with a note written in Doug's handwriting. The other side was blank.

It had the date two weeks from today and below that, two lines which read:

The Downtown Grill
11:30 Violet

I turned it over in case something had somehow magically appeared on the other side since I had first looked at it, but it was still blank.

"What's that?" Mary asked, looking over.

"Oh," I said. "Um, nothing, just someone Doug wanted me to meet."

Mary turned and looked out the window, her mind still full of thoughts of our friends. She would miss Alison tremendously, and while she could still email, calls would be less frequent depending on what the Wallbergs were doing and where they were.

I was certainly going to miss them as well, but my mind was still puzzling over why Doug wanted me to go to this lunch meeting. How was I supposed to find someone named Violet in one of Denver's busiest business lunch restaurants when it would be full of people? Not to mention that the name "Violet" hardly backed up his "It's all in there" remark from when I'd asked who this person was.

More confusing was that Doug had never mentioned that name to me before. Just who was Violet anyway?

Chapter 3
Violet

The next two weeks went by, as they do. Mary went on a business trip to South Carolina, and I went about my days at work with the usual stress, problems, and a never-ending pile of things to do.

I still could not get the dream out of my head. With the winter change in daylight savings time in Colorado, it was always dark when I left the office, and as I drove home, I would look up at the stars in the sky and try to remember the dreams of my youth. I would eventually crawl into bed, exhausted, both mentally and physically. Some days I slept without remembering my LIFE dream, but inevitably I woke up. As often as not, when I looked in the mirror, I was convinced that I would see bruises on my face from the red boxing gloves.

I actually forgot about my lunch appointment until Wednesday came around and I looked at my calendar. There it was: Violet, Downtown Grill, 11:30.

I had only been to the Downtown Grill once before. It was an inappropriately named restaurant in that, although it was indeed downtown, it was not a grill in the traditional sense, but a fine restaurant with white linen tablecloths and impeccable service. Regardless of the time of day, it seemed you always needed a reservation, and there was no name on the building's façade. The street number was simply etched into a glass pane next to the ornate oak front door. This was not something you looked up on the Yelp app. This was a place that catered to the business elite, a place for power lunches, a place where deals got done and private meetings took place.

I walked in, feeling as I had that one time I'd been here before: completely out of place. Although Mary often reminded me that I was now in executive management, I still did not feel like I fit in. I felt guilty every time I charged a lunch to the company, even though they were legitimate lunch meetings. "That's one reason you are such a good manager," was all Mary had said when I had told her once how it made me feel.

Walking in through the dark wooden doors, I found myself at the maître d' station, where a man and woman were standing behind a tall podium, dressed identically in dark pressed slacks, a white shirt and black jacket, and no tie. The woman, a young twenty-something with dark curly hair and an olive complexion, asked if she could help me.

I told her apologetically that I was meeting someone, but I didn't know what she looked like. The woman looked as though this were perfectly normal and asked, "And the name, sir?"

Feeling slightly embarrassed, I said with an air of uncertainty, "Violet?"

Hearing the name, the man looked up from behind the station, his pen in midair. "Ah yes, sir, she has already arrived. This way, please." He was in his mid-fifties, with gray hair and a slight accent. French, perhaps? I wasn't sure.

We walked through the main dining room, which looked very much as expected. Most of the walls were taken up with booths of dark brown wood, with twelve inches of frosted glass partitions above the plush leather seating for privacy. More booths occupied the center of the restaurant, with some tables filling the space in between.

Although the restaurant was almost full, and I could hear the usual melting pot of conversation, clinking glasses, silverware on plates, and the occasional explanation of today's chef's special from servers, the overall sound seemed more like background noise than the ambiance of a busy restaurant.

Dark-framed, glass-enclosed paintings and sketches adorned the walls, depicting country outdoor scenes, architectural abstracts, and here and there a black-and-white photograph of a Denver landmark, as befitting the austerity of the club-like atmosphere.

It seemed as if almost every table and booth were taken, and I scanned the large dining room as we walked, in search of someone that might fit my image of the name "Violet." It was, after all, not a common name in today's society of Miley, Demi, Lindsay, and Brittany.

I spotted a table near the back of the room where an elderly lady was sitting by herself. She wore a cream-colored suit and matching hat with a wide brim. I smiled as we headed in her direction, though she was busy looking down at her menu and not, it seemed, for me.

I was so preoccupied about what to say when I met this mysterious woman that I was totally unprepared for what happened next and almost ran into the back of the maître d'. Fully two tables before we reached the woman in the cream-colored hat, he stopped, turned toward another table, and gestured to an open seat.

After stopping myself mere inches from bowling over him, I turned to the table he was showing me and stared in disbelief at the person seated there. I started to say something to him about there being some mistake, but he cut me off, saying merely, "Enjoy your lunch." Then he turned and walked away.

I turned back toward the table and took in the sight. She was not at all what I had expected. She was in her mid-twenties, if that, with piercings on both sides of her nose and three or four in each ear. Her hair was bright, flaming red: not the color you would typically think of for a redhead, but something akin to fire-engine or candy-apple red. Rather than a professional suit, she wore a sort of flowing short dress full of vibrant reds, blues, greens, yellows, and varying shades of each, with black leggings and black closed-toed flats.

I was still standing there mute when she stood, still chewing a piece of bread. Through her mouthful, she said, "Hi, I'm Violet," and put out her hand.

I managed to regain enough composure to mumble a hello. I said my name was Oliver Goodwin, shook her hand, and then took the seat at the table across from her.

Violet looked across at me and said, "Not what you expected, huh?"

"I'm sorry?" I said, not sure I had heard her correctly.

"Me," she said matter-of-factly, looking around the restaurant, "I'm not what you were expecting."

"Ummm," I said nervously, "well, to be honest . . . no . . . not really."

She didn't seem to take any offense. "Did Dougy tell you anything about me?"

Dougy? I'd never heard him called Dougy before. "No . . . as a matter of fact, he didn't."

She smiled, buttering another piece of bread and taking a bite. She glanced around the room as though she was looking for someone, almost nervously, and yet something about her didn't seem nervous at all. I took in her vivid clothes and her bright red hair and noticed for the first time that she had incredibly bright blue eyes—Paul Newman bright. I could not believe I hadn't noticed her when I walked in. She was so out of place from the regular business crowd in the restaurant, but then my eyes had focused on what I expected to see in the elderly lady, and Violet had been hidden behind one of those frosted glass partitions until we had come around it.

She brought her attention back to me. Her gaze was intensely strong, as though she were looking directly into my soul. "So," she said, "Dougy said you are stressed at work."

I laughed nervously; her directness was unnerving. "Well . . ." I said, "he tends to exaggerate somewhat."

Violet nodded as if she had expected the answer.

I opened my mouth, ready to ask my own question, when the server appeared. He was a young man with short dark hair, impeccably dressed in a yellow jacket and dark slacks. "Miss Violet, I see your guest has arrived." Turning to me, he said, "May I get you something to drink besides water, sir?"

Miss Violet? *She must be a regular here,* I thought. Then I realized that since she stood out so much due to her appearance, of course they would remember her. "No, thank you. Water is fine."

The server went over the daily specials and said he would be back soon to take our orders. Before I could say anything, Violet spoke up. "Tell me, Oliver, how are you sleeping?"

Once again, she was looking directly at me; her bright blue eyes seemed to bore into mine, extracting the answers even before I spoke. "Well," I began. Then, clearing my throat, I said, "I mean, not too bad, I guess."

"Mmmm," she said, nodding. "How many times do you wake up during the night?" Then she began looking around the room again. I took a deep breath, stifling a sigh.

I knew a few people with political aspirations who did that, constantly surveying the room to see who else they might need to talk to. I always felt like they weren't really interested in what I had to say. It had always annoyed me, and I felt the same way now.

"I guess, maybe once or twice a night," I said briskly.

Violet nodded again. The server returned. Violet ordered a buffalo hamburger with fries; I ordered a chicken Caesar salad.

As soon as he left with our orders, Violet, who had once again been looking around the room, returned her gaze to me and said, "How's your wife doing?"

It was unnerving talking with a complete stranger. Yet the way she asked her questions, so frankly and yet so honestly, made me feel compelled to answer her. "Fine," I said.

Then, interrupting her before she could ask another question, I added, "Look, I don't mean to be rude, but I just came here because Doug asked me to. I know nothing about you, who you are, or what you do. I don't even know how you and Doug know each other."

Violet stopped, letting her gaze wander and focused back on me. She was silent for an awkward length of time before she answered. "Dougy and I got together from time to time and talked." Then, as if her answer made all the sense in the world, and even though she hadn't answered my questions at all, she said, "Why do you go to a job you dislike so much?"

I had reached for my water glass to take a drink, and now I sat with it half raised to my mouth, too astonished at her response to complete the task. After a moment, I brought the glass the rest of the way to my mouth and took a drink. I felt my face flush, and I could feel myself becoming defensive. "I actually like my job," I said.

Violet seemed to be interested in something over my left shoulder and tilted her head slightly to look that way.

With her gaze intently on whatever or whomever it was, she said, "You like the job that doesn't let you sleep at night, keeps your blood pressure up, and drains you of the only commodity that has any real value to you?"

The server suddenly appeared with our food. Violet immediately dug into her large buffalo burger, her head constantly swiveling around the room, seemingly looking at everything and nothing simultaneously. Finally, it swiveled my way, and after swallowing her bite, she said, "So what is your passion, Oliver?"

I had just put a forkful of salad into my mouth when she asked the question, and it stopped me cold. I sat there, my mouth full of food, and stared at her for a moment. If she noticed, she certainly did not show it. She ate some French fries and looked around the room again.

I started chewing my food while I tried to understand this strange woman and her illogical process of asking questions. I was still trying to figure out what she had meant by "the only commodity that has any real value to you."

I could not for the life of me figure out what Doug was doing having meetings with such a strange and unique individual. Her mind seemed to be all over the map, and her social skills were practically nonexistent.

The abruptness of her question, however, caused my mind to race. I had been reading books and attending seminars all my life on personal achievement and leadership; certainly, I had made lists of goals and written down dreams on more occasions than I could count. I had read about passion, and it was, in fact, one of my favorite words. Although I had read countless books on goals and dreams over the years, I had never given my passions much thought, much less spoken about them to anyone.

All of this flew through my mind as I finished chewing and put my fork down, grabbing my napkin to wipe my mouth so I could stall a bit longer. I looked up and saw that Violet was staring directly at me once more. As I met her gaze, she simply raised her eyebrows, and I felt my throat tighten.

"I um . . ." I cleared my throat. "Well, I have lots of passions," I said in that vague way people do when they don't know how to respond. I knew as soon as I said it that it was just my own insecurities getting in the way. I was afraid of answering her question. I am not sure I consciously realized it, but looking back, that is exactly what was happening.

"Mmmm," she said, tilting her head to one side as she gazed at me with her piercing blue eyes. "What I am asking, Oliver, is what is your true passion? Your noble purpose? The one thing you believe deep down inside that you were meant to do?"

I felt the jolt of the question run up and down my spine. My body was summoning all its defenses to ward off what was coming. My mind was desperate not to open Pandora's box, because deep down, somewhere in my subconscious, I knew that if I answered the question, I would have to face up to the fact that I had not yet followed my true passion. Worse, I would have to face another truth: that while I may not have answered in my own mind about what my true passion was, there was one thing I knew, without a doubt. That one thing was that although I was good at managing people and working in information technology, the work I had been doing over the last decade and more was most definitely not my true passion.

This was crazy. How could this woman, whom I hardly knew, with her obnoxious questions, her annoying habits, and her inane thought processes, stir up these thoughts and feelings inside of me—and so quickly?

Violet seemed to sense the turmoil in my mind. "That is what I want you to think about before we meet again," she said, taking for granted that this was not a onetime meeting. She had finished most of her meal, while I had barely touched my salad. She reached under the table and grabbed a satchel, which she slung over her shoulder as she stood up.

"Oh, and I think we should meet every week for a while. I think you've wasted enough of that vital commodity called Time, and I think we should focus on getting some things sorted, don't you?" She offered her hand.

I stood up clumsily and shook it, nodding slightly without saying anything. I was still so dumbfounded by her question, I couldn't quite process what she was saying until she was already walking away. I watched as she approached the maître d' station. Several people turned and stared as she walked by their tables, but she was oblivious to them. When she reached the maître d', he stopped talking to the couple he had been attending to and gave her a hug, each of them kissing the other on both cheeks like they do in Europe, and then she was gone. I would learn later that she had paid the bill ahead of time.

I sat at the table for a long time, picking at my salad but not really tasting it. I thought about this strange woman whom I knew nothing more about now than when I came in, other than what she looked like. I tried to remember our conversation and realized I had done most of the talking and she had simply asked questions. Talk about the quintessential "How to Win Friends and Influence People" technique; she had it down cold. Most of all, I stared into space and tried to remember her words.

What I'm asking, Oliver, is what is your true passion, your noble purpose, the one thing you believe deep down inside that you were meant to do?

I sat there for the better part of an hour. I thought about all the possible answers to that question. I tried to come up with the best one, the one that truly got to my heart.

I knew I had to tap into my emotions. I had to tap into that part of me that would come alive and cause my heart to race, but as I sat there, only one emotion stood out. It was strong and fervent, clamoring for attention, and had an equally pulse-racing effect. I almost gasped out loud when I realized what it was.

It was fear!

Chapter 4
Passion

By the time I returned to my office, I already had an email from Violet with a calendar appointment for lunch every week for the next twelve weeks. I stared at my computer screen for quite some time, wondering whether I should accept it. My mind was in some sort of fog, not quite able to function. The drive back from lunch was a blur; I couldn't even remember being in the car.

Now, here I was in my office, staring at this email from a woman I had just met. A woman with peculiar habits and even more peculiar dress, whose questions were banging around in my head like some runaway pinball with no exit lane.

I watched, almost as if from across the room, as my right hand reached for the mouse. My index finger was poised as I smoothly glided the pointer over the button on the screen. The click, when I pressed down on the button, seemed deafening in my ears, adding to the clanging cacophony her questions had caused in my mind. I watched as the "accept" button on the screen depressed, and the screen switched to my calendar to show the appointment scheduled for next week.

I was exhausted when I arrived home that night, and for once, I beat Mary to bed, falling asleep almost as soon as my head hit the pillow. My dreams were bizarre, somewhat macabre, as if someone from Cirque du Soleil had put on a show about my life. I woke up far from refreshed, and though I could not remember one way or the other, my body felt as though the red gloves had had their way with me again. I headed to the office. I just couldn't get the questions out of my head.

What is your true passion? Your noble purpose?

The one thing you believe deep down inside that you were meant to do.

I found my attention slipping in meetings. I would spend fifteen, twenty, sometimes forty-five minutes at a time gazing off into the distance while I sat in my office. It was not my finest day at work.

When the evening arrived, I wearily dragged myself in from the garage, and when Mary saw me, the look on her face changed from joy to concern.

"Oliver," she exclaimed. "You look exhausted."

I smiled weakly. "Sorry, it's been a long week."

We talked over dinner about our days. She expressed concern again about my long hours at work and the stress she said was clearly written all over my face.

That night, as we got ready for bed, I told her about Violet. Mary was riveted by my story of how Doug had asked me to meet with Violet and my description of our unusual first meeting.

"So, you don't know who she is or how Doug knows her?" she asked.

"None."

"Why don't you just ask him?"

"I did," I answered. "I mean, I tried."

"What do you mean, you tried?"

"Well, I tried calling him, but all I got was his voicemail."

"Yeah," she said, "they have been hard to get a hold of since they arrived. I only got to talk to Alison once, and that was for five minutes."

"I know," I said, "and I know they have a busy schedule right now getting settled in and everything, so I sent him an email."

"And?" Mary prompted.

"And nothing." I shook my head. "All he said in his reply was that she was an old friend and that the lunches would do me good."

"That seems vague," Mary admitted.

"Tell me about it. Not to mention they can't be that old of friends—the woman has to be half his age." Then I added with a smile, "Half our age."

We talked about what my lunch with Violet was like, what she was wearing, how she acted. We tried to guess her background and what connection she could have to Doug.

"You don't think Violet is Doug's . . . what . . . girlfriend . . . mistress . . . illegitimate daughter?" Mary asked incredulously.

"No," I blurted. "No, I just . . . oh, I don't know, she is just . . . I can't put my finger on it, honey, but I don't think it's anything like that."

Mary thought about it for a minute and then said, "Yeah . . . maybe you're right. Why don't you just ask Violet?"

"I tried," I said defensively. "I just couldn't."

Mary half frowned and half smirked. "You couldn't?"

"I can't explain it. You had to be there. She doesn't give you much of a chance to ask questions, just to answer them."

"What kind of questions?"

I ran through most of our conversation for Mary and paused when I got to the end.

"What's the matter?" Mary asked, noticing the strange look on my face as I recalled the end of our conversation.

I looked at her, all the insecurities and fear that I had felt at the table in the restaurant returning. "She asked me a question I couldn't answer," I said, afraid of speaking even those words out loud.

"What question?" Mary asked, a puzzled look on her face. "She asked me what my passion was."

Mary sat back with a look I could not quite place, somewhere between curiosity and surprise. Then she looked me straight in the eye, and with that "now you listen to me" voice, she said, "Oliver Goodwin, that is a question you had better figure out how to answer. And I mean right now!"

I knew I should have said nothing. Mary was my biggest fan, but she was also the one person who did not let me slide on anything. It was one of the many reasons I loved her and looked up to her so much. She had this ability to get me to think about and do things I did not want to do. She was a determined woman—when she set her mind to something, there was no changing it, and now she had set her mind on me.

I was in big trouble.

We talked for hours. Mary was too smart for me. She would let me dance around it for a while, knowing me better than I even knew myself, but she kept bringing me back until I finally homed in on the actual answer.

"Spit it out, Oliver!" she said finally. "You and I both know what it is. You have been skirting the edge of it for the past hour. It's obvious. Why are you so afraid to say it?"

I looked at her, at her amazingly beautiful face, at the kindness in her eyes and the warmth of her smile. I could never lie to her. "I'm scared," I said simply.

"What?" she said, truly taken aback. "I have never known you to fear anything." Then she reached out and took my hand in hers. "Honey, you are the one who taught me to face up to my fears. That there is nothing we can't do together, right?" She smiled that amazing smile of hers again. "Weren't you the one who told me I can do anything I set my mind to?"

I nodded slowly.

"Well, buster," she said, her smile turning serious, "you need to listen to your own words, because there is nothing, and I mean nothing, that you cannot do." She paused, but her eyes never left mine. "You are the most amazing man I have ever known. And I am telling you right now that whatever you want to do, truly want to do, you can do. I believe in you."

I felt myself welling up a little and tried to laugh it off. And then, with a sudden surge of confidence that her words had given me, I said in a quick rush of words that felt like they were too hot on my tongue, "I want to write a book!"

She smiled that smile again, the one that could light up most of Colorado if we could figure out how to connect it to the grid.

"I want to write, and I want to help people," I said truthfully. And then I dropped my head as I felt all the thoughts and fears come charging back.

"But?" she said, knowing all too well what I was thinking. I looked up at her again. After a lengthy pause, I tried a halfhearted smile. "But," I said, "I don't really have anything new to say, much less to help people with."

Mary straightened and brought herself to her full height in what I liked to tease her was her "teacher" pose. "Excuse me?" she said with about as much sarcasm as I had ever heard her use. "Everything you teach me is stuff I never knew existed. Nothing new to write about, are you kidding me?"

"Honey, you don't read the same books I do. All the stuff I talk about is just what I've read. It's nothing new," I countered.

"And what do you think those authors you read wrote about? You think they came up with all that stuff by themselves?" she asked incredulously.

"Well . . . yeah," I said.

"I'm sorry," Mary continued, "but aren't you the same Oliver Goodwin who has been telling me that these books go back for centuries, some even to Roman philosophers? That the real 'secret' to success is found in the classic authors you like so much?"

"Yeah," was all I could say.

"Well then, none of those best-selling authors you read have been writing anything new, have they?" Before I could answer, she kept going. "It's not about saying anything new, honey. If the true principles of what is out there have always held true, the way you tell me they have, then finding something new isn't the goal. The goal is to say it in a way that is relevant today. Finding your own voice to help tell people about these principles in a way that makes sense to them, in a way that only you can."

She wasn't finished. "I have never heard of the things you've taught me, and I guarantee that most people out there haven't either. I certainly haven't read all those books, and I'll bet most of the people we know haven't either. Don't you sell yourself short, honey—what you have to say is important, and a lot of people need to hear it."

I had no idea she felt that way. I had always thought the stuff I talked about from all the books I'd read over the years was obvious. Those ideas certainly seemed obvious to me, but as we talked, she pointed out that it was only because I knew them. They hadn't been obvious to me until I read them.

Not for the first time in my life, I reminded myself of why I loved Mary so much.

We went to bed far too late, but I slept fitfully. And although the specter of fear at having found my passion and noble purpose still ran around in my head, there was also something new. Somewhere in there, lurking in the shadows, perhaps, but there nonetheless, was a tiny spark of a feeling. I wasn't quite sure what it was. Conviction maybe? Relief? Whatever it was, it was a good feeling, and the more I thought about writing and helping people, the stronger the feeling grew.

Chapter 5
What to Write

The next day at work was hectic. I had let too many things pile up, and I delved into the emails, reports, meetings, and strategy sessions with renewed vigor. Something had changed inside of me, almost as if a weight had been lifted from my shoulders.

By Friday afternoon, I had a break in the tidal wave of things to do, and as I sat at my desk, looking out the window at the peaks in the distance, my gaze fell toward the buildings, houses, and trees that made up the miles of landscape between my office and those majestic mountains.

I suddenly thought of all the people in those homes and buildings and wondered if there was a way my book could help them. My mind immediately filled with the usual suspect: doubt. Who was I to think I could write something that others would want to read? Was I really arrogant enough to believe that what I had to say could actually make a difference in people's lives?

After a good thirty minutes of self-pity and loathing, my internal demons switched tack, and I wondered just what I would write about, never mind that no one would want to read it. The rest of the day was a mixture of small bouts of work interspersed with periods of self-doubt. By the time I packed up my bag and headed to my car, the sun was sinking along with my mood. I was ready to give up on the whole crazy idea.

I decided not to share my thoughts with Mary. I knew it would only make her dig her heels in, and she would dedicate herself to changing my mind. I spent the weekend doing chores, catching up on some work, and trying to fight the battle in my mind between my dream and what I thought of as my reality. Every time I tried to think of an idea for what to write about, I found ten reasons why the idea was futile. Once or twice, I thought I had stumbled upon a workable solution, only to find myself shooting it full of holes.

I kept coming back to the initial idea I'd had years ago. Although I thought no one had really done what I wanted to do, I could not exactly come to the point of convincing myself that it was of any value. I finally gave in Sunday afternoon, my mind numb from the voices of doubt in my head. I spent the evening relaxing with Mary, watching a new mystery on PBS and then going to bed for the first time in days without thinking about the idea of writing a book.

I arrived a little early for my lunch with Violet on Monday, but as I was being shown to the table, I could see she was already there. Still the same red hair, but this time she wore a bright red cape that made her look like Little Red Riding Hood. It was spectacular, and like the week before, people were staring. Also as before, Violet didn't seem to care or notice. She simply looked around and smiled when she caught someone looking.

"Hello," she said as I approached.

"Hi," I replied, and as I opened my mouth, determined to ask my own questions this time, she looked down at her menu and said, "Gerald said the special today is salmon in a lemon butter sauce with capers. I think I might try that. It sounds good."

"Gerald?" I asked.

She looked up at me. "Yeah . . . Gerald." Then, with a tone suggesting that everyone knew who Gerald was, she added, "The maître d'?"

Slapping the menu down on the table with her palm, she looked across at me and said, "So?"

Surprised yet again, I said, "So? Um . . . I don't know, I'm not a big fan of salmon."

Violet once again looked around the room. This time she spoke while her head was still turned to the side, toward the entrance. "I am not talking about the menu. Your passion. Did you find it?"

A server arrived to take our order, saving me from growling with frustration. Violet ordered the special; I had a bowl of soup and a turkey sandwich.

Violet seemed to have a talent for annoying me. Not just by the way she looked around when she talked or when I was talking, but also because she heard everything I said, and sometimes even what I wasn't saying.

I took a piece of bread for myself and aggressively buttered it, pressing down too hard with the knife, so it practically tore through the soft white center.

"So, what did you figure out?"

Although I could not quite pinpoint why, I was angry, so I answered her emotionally, my jaw tight and my voice rising slightly. "Maybe I'm doing my noble purpose right now. Maybe my passion is taking care of the people in my department at work and making lives better for those we ultimately serve with the technology we're developing?"

Violet broke off a piece of bread and held it up to her mouth. As she opened her mouth to put it in, she said simply, "Nope."

I put my knife down forcefully, clanging it on the side of my plate and drawing a few looks from the tables nearby. I leaned forward and, in a low but firm voice, said, "How do you know? You know nothing about me."

After taking a sip from her water, she looked at me as if I had just asked her the time of day and said calmly, "Because if you were doing your noble purpose or you had already followed your passion, you would have been able to answer the question last week when I asked it."

It was infuriating. I couldn't even argue with her logic. I wanted to laugh at the absurd truth of it all. How was this twenty-something girl with bright hair, piercing blue eyes, and wild clothes so perceptive?

Once again, I found myself wondering, *who is she?*

"Tell me." She said, breaking my thoughts. "I won't laugh, I promise."

There was something in the way she said it, like an innocent child exchanging secrets with her best friend. I realized I felt completely at ease telling her. I knew she was telling the truth, and that she was interested in the answer. I didn't know how I knew. I just knew.

It came out almost before I knew what I was saying. "I want to be an author. I want to write a book that helps people."

"Helps them do what?" she asked immediately. No judgment, just a question.

The server arrived with our food, giving me a little time to compose the answer.

"I'm not sure," I replied after the server left. "I'm thinking about writing about the best self-achievement books to read that have the core principles to make people successful, with additional suggestions for people who want to delve deeper into each principle at the end of each chapter."

Violet pursed her lips. "Interesting," she said. "A book about reading books."

"It's more than that," I said defensively. I was annoyed by her straightforward simplification of everything I said. "It would be kind of like a university for people who really want to better their lives. It would help them get started by learning the basics, and then they could read more if they wanted to study something more in-depth. Sort of like continued education for those who wanted their master's or PhD."

I watched as Violet took a bite of her salmon and looked around the room. Gathering steam in my defense, I continued. "Look, when I started reading, I didn't know which books to read. There are so many books on success and personal achievement, not to mention business, management, and leadership strategy. I've read and studied literally hundreds of books. This will help people who don't know where to start."

She brought her gaze back to me, her eyes once again boring into my soul. I could almost feel the intense heat behind my retinas. "Well, at least you're passionate about it."

I could feel every muscle in my body tighten. "Why did you ask if you don't believe my answer? I've thought a lot about this and I really do want to be an author. I think this is a good idea for a book."

Violet looked at me with a blank expression on her face. I had no idea what she was thinking. She stared at me for what seemed like a long time. She didn't seem in the least bit affected by the tone of my voice or my accusatory tone. Her expression was almost inquisitive. Finally, she blinked, looked down at her knife and fork as she speared another piece of salmon, and said, "I know people. I've been studying them for a long time. I don't doubt you want to be an author, but this is not your book."

I wanted to scream. I wanted to shout at her, "How do you know?" But I just sat across from her, speechless.

"Still," she said, pushing some rice onto her fork with her knife, "you definitely are closer than you were last week. Keep going, you'll get there."

If I hadn't known better, I would have taken that comment as condescending, but looking at her, I knew Violet had not meant it that way at all. She was just . . . *Just what?* I thought. *Just being Violet* popped into my head. Yes, that was it. She was just a young, brash, very blunt girl. She said what she meant and meant what she said.

I thought, *wouldn't it be nice if more people were like that?* I looked down at my sandwich and noticed that I was much less frustrated than I had been a few moments ago. Why was that?

I went home late again that night, and I didn't have a chance to talk to Mary about my conversation with Violet until we were both ready for bed.

After I had recapped my conversation with Violet, Mary said, "You know, honey, just because Violet says something doesn't mean she is right."

"I know," I said, putting my shoes away and climbing into bed. "But . . ." I started.

"But what?" Mary plugged her phone into its charger on her nightstand.

I sighed loudly. "I don't know . . . she really bugs me . . . but . . ."

Mary kept looking at me, waiting.

I looked over at her. "I can't explain it, honey. It's something about the way she says things . . . and . . . well . . . maybe she is right."

"But I thought you've been wanting to write this book for a long time?" Mary said.

"I have, but that's just it. I *have* wanted to do it for a long time, but I've always felt like it wasn't really enough. Like the idea was not really what I wanted or not quite right somehow. I don't know, I've been thinking about it and how I would write it, and the more I think about it the more complicated it gets, and it all seems overwhelming . . . just getting it down on paper."

"Remember, sweetheart," Mary said as she leaned over to turn out her bedside light, "eating an elephant can only happen one bite at a time."

I smiled and leaned in to kiss her before I laid down to go to sleep. It did not come easy, but at some point I finally drifted off. I dreamed about Violet following me everywhere I went. Her red hair and long red cape flowed behind her as her piercing blue eyes bore into mine and told me over and over that I was writing the wrong book. Each time I turned around trying to flee from her, LIFE was standing there blocking my way, feet planted, with his red boxing gloves on. I would gasp just before the red blur of LIFE's right jab hit me and spun me around, only to face Violet once more with her incessant rebuke.

It was a long night.

Chapter 6
Double Helix

Gerald looked up from behind his podium when I walked in the following week. He peered over his rimless spectacles at the sound of my approach. Although he did not actually smile, there was a pleasant enough look of recognition as he put down his pen and emerged from behind his protective barrier. "Good morning, Mr. Goodwin." And with his customary wave of the hand, he added, "This way to your table, sir."

That garnered a few raised eyebrows from the waiting patrons just inside the door. I smiled to myself as I followed him, convinced that my third trip in as many weeks to his restaurant was not what had garnered me "your table" status. No, it was probably my dining companion that had elevated me in his eyes.

Although we didn't sit at the same table each week, this time we were sitting where I had first met the still-mysterious Violet. Today she had cut her hair shorter and wore it sticking up in all directions. It was still bright red, and the overall effect was of a tomato in mid-explosion sitting on top of her oval face.

Gerald escorted me to my seat, and with a polite nod to Violet, he returned to his station—no doubt to deal with patrons who were not on the "your table" list.

I was determined this time not to let Violet command the conversation.

"OK," I started. "Maybe you were right about... what did you call it, a book about reading books?"

Violet looked at me with her intensely blue eyes and nodded.

"I've been doing a lot of thinking, trying to figure out what it is I want to write about, and I just can't figure it out."

Violet nodded, as though that made perfect sense to her. She did her usual scan around the room as she thought about whatever she thought about, and then she said, "Why do you want to write?"

That was easy. "I want to help people."

"Help them do what?" she countered. She looked straight at me before glancing around the room once again. Although it still annoyed me when she did that, I found I wasn't as bothered by it as I had been when we first met.

I didn't pause this time; the answer just sort of came out. "I want to help people live better lives."

This brought her attention back quickly. Her eyes piercing mine, she leaned forward and said, "What does that mean, help people live better lives?"

It was my turn to lean in this time. "I've been reading books for as long as I can remember," I said. "You know, all the classic self-help books, the new thinking philosophy books, and business books, everything from goal setting to the Law of Attraction to how to build relationships and find happiness."

I moved my plate to the side so I could lean my arms on the table as I continued. "They're all great books. I mean, I learned something from all of them, and I definitely have put many of those principles into practice in my life and career. I guess that's why I had that idea of writing a list of books people should read, but it would never work. I've been reading those books for decades; no one has that kind of time now."

I took a sip of water as Violet looked on. "The thing is," I said, "I can't quite get my head around some things. First, I always had a hard time identifying with some of these people. They are already successful, so it's easy for them to say 'do this' or 'do that.' What about the guy who's just starting out? Where's his example?" I was getting into it now, and my voice was getting higher with excitement. "Plus," I continued, "If everyone reads the next brilliant book on success or the timeless classic from way back, how come everyone isn't successful?"

"Good point," Violet said.

"There has to be something missing," I said, throwing up my hands. "I want to help people be successful no matter what area they want to be successful at in their lives and no matter what stage they are at in their success." I was leaning so far over the table that people at the table next to us were glancing over, but I didn't care.

"I want to find a way to help people *live a better life!*" I finished, emphasizing those last words individually.

Violet just smiled back at me. She wasn't looking around the room. She was looking right back at me, her face half the width of the table away. "Sounds like you've found your passion."

I sat back in my seat and took a deep breath. Then I looked at her and smiled.

We spent the rest of the lunch talking about what might be missing. Well, I did most of the talking and, as usual, Violet mostly asked questions.

As lunch began winding down, I asked, "How did you know I wasn't living my passion when you first asked me?"

Violet paused, looking around the room in her way before answering. "Because people don't talk about what they are good at or how long they have been doing something when they talk about their passion. When they talk about something they are truly passionate about, they get excited." Her speech became louder and faster, her arms moving about, mimicking what I had been doing earlier in our lunch. "They can't stop telling you all the things they want to do or are looking forward to." She leaned back in her chair and then calmly said, "When I originally asked you, you just sat there and talked about things you did at your job like you were watching paint dry."

For the rest of the week, I wrote down ideas. I would get home after work and pull some books from my bookshelves, flipping through them and writing the principles or primary thoughts the authors expressed. I was trying to find the common threads. I found several and began making notes. At lunch, I would close my office door and sort through my thoughts, trying to organize them into coherent themes. My notes grew longer.

The following Monday, I arrived at lunch and sat down with Violet, whose hair had now turned purple to match the floral-patterned dress she was wearing. Spring was still a few weeks away, but we were enjoying an unusual early warm-up from winter this year, and I suppose it inspired Violet to break out her spring fashions.

"Hi," she said by way of greeting as I sat down. "How did it go this week?"

"Well," I said, bringing out my notebook and opening to the first page, "I don't know. I think I'm onto something, but it's kind of all over the place."

"Show me," she said, and so I did.

I went through my notes as we ordered our lunch and picked at our food. She asked lots of questions, and by the end, I had diagrammed the primary principles I had found as themes. "It's like I'm trying to build a chain," I said.

"More like a double helix," Violet countered. "Almost like DNA."

"Yes!" I said excitedly. "I could call it the DNA of Success."

We finished with at least a rough draft written across two pages of my notebook, and I committed to flushing out this DNA of Success by the following week. I left the room feeling better than I ever had about the direction I was heading in. Gerald even raised an eyebrow as I hummed and waved goodbye on my way out.

My elation was short-lived.

I went home that night, took out a piece of drawing paper, and mapped out the DNA of Success. I started with the core principles and then added all the influencing factors I could think of. I sat in my den chair until almost eleven, rifling through volumes of books as I searched for the key ingredients of success.

I did it again the following night, as Mary was once again on a trip. Marlow, my ever-faithful companion, sat by my feet as I frantically searched for missing pieces of the puzzle.

By Thursday, I began to feel discouraged. The diagram was getting out of control. Lines connected and intersected from one principle to another (and yet another), to the point that I was beginning to lose track of which were core principles and which were supporting ones.

When Mary came home Friday, she found me in my den chair with papers strewn all over the floor. Even Marlow was afraid to come in, and even if he hadn't been, there was nowhere for him to sit.

"It looks like a trash can exploded in here," Mary said.

I sighed heavily and told her all about my DNA of Success and my failure in trying to create it.

She ran her hand down the back of my head and said gently, "OK, honey. Why don't you take a break?" She helped me out of the chair and down into the kitchen. "Let's get something to eat. When was the last time you ate?"

I mumbled something about breakfast, and she soon began gathering pots and pans and throwing some food together for us. I sat on the couch and wondered where I had gone wrong with the DNA model.

We spent the weekend catching up on household chores. For the first time in a long time, I had trouble sleeping again. LIFE was back, and though he wasn't assaulting me head-on, he followed me everywhere I went, his red-gloved hands shoving me this way and that, punching me in the shoulder if I turned the wrong way. He was incessant, relentless, and unforgiving, but the alleyways and side streets I walked down from one to the next never ended. I was in a labyrinth that had no exit. I woke up exhausted and with more than a few sore muscles in my arms and shoulders.

Chapter 7
Defining Success

Violet took one look at me on Monday and said, "What's wrong?"

I sank down heavily into my side of the booth and replied, "Everything."

Violet waited, not saying a word and looking around the room as always. I reached into my notebook and pulled out the folded piece of drawing paper with the puzzle of the DNA of Success model I had been working on. I set it down unceremoniously on the table, and she unfolded it and laid it out in front of her.

I watched as she cocked her head from side to side, reading the various scribbles I had made to connect one principle to another. Finally, she looked up at me and raised an eyebrow.

"I know, I know," I said defensively, already expecting the admonition she was going to give me.

"What do you know?" she asked.

I gestured at the paper. "It's ridiculous!"

She took a quick survey of the room and then said, "It's complicated. It's perhaps a little confusing. It's not ridiculous."

I looked at her in surprise. "But there's no way I can use this," I protested.

"Maybe," she answered. "Maybe there's something here." Why was it that every time I thought I was right about something, she always took the opposite point of view?

"What if this is simply too involved?" she asked, then followed with, "What if there's something in here, but it's hidden amongst all the various connections? Is it possible there's a truth in here that's right in front of your nose, but you can't see it because of all the noise?"

I was still skeptical and told her so through some mumbling and gestures, but when she turned the paper around to face me, I looked at it.

She leaned over it a little, the color of her shirt a sharp contrast against the white paper. She was in full spring mode today, with a lime green shirt, brown pants, and her still-purple hair. "How would you boil this down if you could only list four or five main points?" Before I could even think of an answer, she said, "And what is the goal that they lead to?"

"What do you mean, the goal? The goal is success, of course!" I replied indignantly.

She leaned back into her side of the booth. "Success," she said. "And just what is success?"

I opened my mouth to answer, but found I didn't quite know what to say. "Well . . . um . . ." I stammered.

She was in a playful mood today. Her tone of voice was now taunting as she looked around. "Is success the same for everyone?"

"No, of course not."

"Are you sure?"

I frowned, now unsure of anything. What had been a lousy week of trying to dissect the DNA of Success was turning into an ugly Monday lunch. "Yes," I said, half believing it. "Success is different for everyone."

"Why?"

"Because everyone wants something different. Because everyone is at a different place in their lives, and their goals and dreams are unique." I was confident now, and I looked at her defiantly as her gaze swept back around the room and rested on me.

"OK," she said, "everyone wants something different." Tilting her head to the right, she added, "But why do they want it?"

"Why?" I asked incredulously. "What do you mean, why do they want it?"

Infuriatingly, she asked me another question. "Don't you want to help people no matter where they are in life?"

I nodded, so she added, "And don't you want to help people no matter what their dreams and goals are?"

"Yes," I said, getting impatient. "So?"

"So," she said, "If everyone you want to help has different goals and dreams—is at different stages in their lives—this nebulous goal of 'success' can't be the end of the path you want to help them to, can it?"

As her words sank in, I felt myself dropping even further into despair. *Great,* I thought. *Now I can't even use the DNA of Success model because there is no end goal.*

Violet was watching me intently. Again, she asked, "Why do they want whatever it is they want?"

I threw my hands up. "How should I know?"

"Why does anyone want success?"

"I don't know—more money, more power, more security, I guess."

"And why do they want that?"

I was really getting tired of her incessant questions, but as I looked up into her innocent blue eyes, I couldn't find a reason to be angry. So I asked myself, *Why would anyone want something, anything?* I filtered it through my head, trying to find the ultimate reason. I kept asking "why" again and again, and ultimately, I found it.

I suddenly looked up at her from my musing and said, "They want to be happy."

Violet smiled, and I felt like I had just answered the teacher's question with the right answer. Part of me wondered fleetingly why I felt Violet was a teacher, but her voice brought my mind back to the task at hand.

"So," she said, "if the goal is to be happy, what four or five points from this . . ."—she paused as she searched for the right word, looking down at my diagram—". . . model . . . would you be able to use to explain to me how to achieve it?"

We ordered and ate our food, going back and forth over the DNA paper the whole time. It was an amazing experience as we dissected each tenant, each principle of success, examining the pros and cons and deciding if it was indeed a core principle or a supporting one and ultimately deciding whether it helped someone get closer to their goal or moved them further away.

The restaurant was almost empty by the time we finished. Only three other tables had anyone sitting at them. Our server had given up asking if we wanted refills, as we had already paid the check. She was too polite to ask us to leave and, of course, would never hover over us. This was, after all, the Denver Grill.

Violet and I had boiled my idea down to four core principles. The first was ACTION. Actions ultimately determined if someone got closer to or further from their goal or dream. FOCUS then determined someone's actions, since the things a person focused on regularly would determine what actions they chose. THOUGHTS were next, as what someone thinks about will determine what they focus on. Finally, we identified the INTERNAL CONVERSATION, that personal dialogue we all have going on in our minds, which determines our thoughts.

We had found the core DNA. INTERNAL CONVERSATION drives THOUGHTS, which drive FOCUS, which drives ACTIONS, which ultimately determine success. Success, of course, ultimately boils down to being happy.

I was jazzed. Violet had done it again. She had helped me overcome the obstacles in my head, and together we had defined the core principles that would drive my writing. I couldn't wait to get home so I could begin. I was so excited I wanted to kiss her, and when she stood up with her satchel to leave, I also rose and looked at her. She looked back blankly and cocked her head a little. I felt awkward and didn't know quite what to do. It was silly; I was a teenager in high school all over again, unsure of what to say or do.

"Thank you," I said simply, holding out my hand.

She looked at it for a moment, as if surprised by the gesture. Then she took my hand and shook it, saying, "I can't make our meeting next Monday, but I'll see you in two weeks." And with that, she walked around me and headed for the front of the restaurant.

I was disappointed that I wouldn't see her for two weeks. We had made so much progress, but then I realized I could start writing now, and two weeks gave me time to make some real headway in the book. I left once again feeling like I was on cloud nine, though this time Gerald was not at his podium as I walked by to give me his raised eyebrow.

After dinner, I headed up to my attic-den and sat down to write. Mary said she needed to work on a presentation for an upcoming client trip, which suited me fine. I had done some research on how to write, and while some blogs and articles conflicted with each other or offered differing advice, I applied what made sense to me and let go of the rest.

I started out with a rough outline, giving chapters loose headings and then putting subheadings under them. I was trying to put together the framework of the book so I wouldn't have to think about what to write next.

It took me until late into the night to do it, and I was exhausted when I looked back at my work. It was pretty good, I thought. Not quite right. There was still some tweaking to do, that I could tell, but overall it was a good start.

I went to bed after eleven and slept mostly through the night. LIFE didn't interrupt my dreams, though unfinished things at the office began creeping into my subconscious. Twice, I woke up worrying about deadlines that were coming up and the mountain of work that never seemed to get smaller.

I spent the rest of the week trying to focus on my job and attacking some of the heavy workload I was managing, and in my spare time, mostly at night, I wrote. Some of the writing flowed easily; some of it was challenging. Whenever I became frustrated, I would tell myself to leave that section or chapter and work on another, and I would move on to something that came to me a little more readily.

By the following week, I had written something in about half the chapters and had struggled in the others, but I was making progress. It was about halfway through that second week I hit my first "writer's block." Not that I couldn't think of what to write next. It was that I got a feeling that something was wrong; something was missing. Try as I might, I couldn't move past it. I spent the rest of the week and all weekend going over and over it in my mind.

Sunday night, LIFE came back. He was playing a menacing game of hide and seek with me in which, if he found me, it meant getting pummeled by those red boxing gloves and his dangerous left hook. I stayed hidden most of the way, and it was just as he had discovered my hiding place and was advancing toward me that I woke up on Monday morning, grateful to escape the dream. I was exhausted from my lack of restful sleep.

Mary was worried. She said I had tossed and turned all night, mumbling. She added I had been doing it for most of the past month.

I was sure she was mistaken. Things were mostly going well with the book, except of course the last few days, and work wasn't that bad, was it?

Chapter 8
Jumping Off The Cliff

I spent most of Monday morning dealing with fires at work and mulling over my writer's block. I was trying to figure out what was wrong, what was bugging me, what could be missing.

I was looking forward to seeing Violet again, and as I drove downtown and found a place to park, I kept wondering if she could help me break through this new hurdle. As I walked to the restaurant, I tried to imagine what she would wear this time. I also wondered what she would say after I told her how much progress I had made and how it had come to a screeching halt last week.

I dutifully followed Gerald as he led me into the restaurant. Neither of us needed words by this point. He would simply nod and lead the way, and I would follow. I wondered what questions Violet would ask me and if they would help me figure out what I was missing.

It was that last thought that was running through my mind as I approached the table. This time, Violet wore a comfortable-looking yellow blouse and sported bleached blond hair. Just as I was about to sit down, it hit me. It was as powerful as one of LIFE's punches, but far less painful.

I felt as though someone had smacked the side of my head, and I felt that moment when all the dizziness dissipates, and clarity returns. Like holding your breath underwater and finally being able to breathe again when you break the surface.

Violet looked like she was waiting for me to respond to something she had said, but I just looked at her and stood by my chair. "That's it!" I mumbled.

"What's it?"

Of course it would be a question that I first heard from her. "Questions!" I said, and then I added, "They're the answer."

As if that made all the sense in the world.

"Maybe you should back up and tell me what you've been doing," she said, picking up her menu and looking at me over it.

I told her about all the writing and how last week I had gotten stuck. I told her about how I'd been thinking through every angle all week and all weekend, trying to figure out what was wrong.

"And what *was* wrong?" she asked.

"It occurred to me," I said, "that we didn't finish the core principles." She cocked an eye at me before glancing around the room. I no longer worried about her glances, as I knew she was still listening, so I went on, "You see, we said that the internal dialogue determines someone's thoughts, and that's right. I then assumed that we just needed to help someone make sure they kept the internal dialogue pointed in the right direction. You know, positive thinking, mantras, that sort of thing."

Violet nodded, so I continued. "What was bugging me was that if what I just said is true, then why doesn't it work for everyone?"

That got her attention, and she brought her wandering gaze back to me.

"That's when I started thinking that something was missing. There had to be something that helps successful people drive their internal dialogue where unsuccessful people don't."

"Makes sense," Violet said as I paused.

I leaned closer. "It's questions." I waited to see her reaction, but she simply stared back at me. "Don't you see?" I said, smiling. "It was all those questions you keep asking me that finally helped me figure it out. We all ask ourselves questions all the time. Everything we say and do is in response to questions we're asking ourselves from the moment we wake until we go to bed at night."

Violet leaned back in her chair and smiled, and again I felt the flutter inside of a little boy having done well. We talked through it over the rest of our lunch. No need to stay too late this time; we were back on track. I was back on track. She looked over my outline and made one or two suggestions. She asked me to email her what I had already written and said she would read it during the week. Meanwhile, I committed to moving on now that I was armed with the missing piece of the puzzle.

I couldn't wait to keep writing. I knew I was onto something, and I was excited to get it down on paper.

My sleep, however, was not improving. While I no longer fought with LIFE in my dreams, I couldn't get through the night without waking up at least once in a cold sweat, my mind racing with worries about my workload and the employees in my department. My job was no more or less difficult than anyone else in my position at companies the world over. We had the same amount of drama, office politics, and trouble to deal with. For whatever reason, it was all coming to a head at the worst possible moment.

It happened Friday night—Saturday morning, to be precise.

I went to bed around eleven o'clock, having put the finishing touches on yet another chapter in the book that still didn't have a title but was coming along. I fell asleep quickly, as it had been a long, rotten week at work and the late nights of writing were taking their toll.

Life was back: menacing, angry, and relentless as ever.

I was on the beach again, this time gazing in wonder at the stars in the dark but clear blue sky. I felt at peace, looking up at the blinking lights and marveling at how many there were, how incredible it was to see them, and . . .

Something crossed my vision. It was fleeting, but for a moment, the star I was looking at vanished. It was back now, but as I turned to look at another, there was something blocking it again. One moment the star was there, and the next it was gone.

It took me a moment to realize that clouds were moving across the sky. They were small and wispy, but as they moved across my vision, they would block out the star I was gazing at, even if only for a moment.

I was so focused on wondering why the clouds were blocking my view that I never saw it coming. So intent was my gaze that my mind never even registered the danger until it was too late. The red glove filled my immediate field of vision in a blur as Life, standing tall above my head where I lay on the sand, had reached down and was aiming his fist straight at me. I winced, thinking the blow would strike my head, but that was not his target.

The pain was immediate and violent. Life had gone down on one knee as his punch neared its target, turning as he did to put the full weight of his shoulder into the blow. It landed on the left side of my chest.

It wasn't the impact that knocked the wind out of me as much as the pain that spread like a typhoon, which left no muscle able to expand my lungs. I couldn't breathe.

I opened my eyes and tried to scream in horror as I saw the red-gloved hand and the arm retract and then come crashing down once more into the same spot, but no sound escaped my lips. Lightning flashed across my vision, though I knew my eyes were now closed. The explosions of light were a reflection of my nervous system's circuitry, which flashed panicked alarms as my body went into shock.

Once again, I opened my eyes, and it was as if this mere act was a signal that my body should somehow respond. I tried to breathe. The simple effort of my lungs trying to expand sent a whole new meaning of pain throughout my body. I knew in that moment that I was going to die.

Life was upright now, menacingly pacing around me, moving from one side, around my feet, to the other, only to reverse direction and do it again. He was furious; it was written all over his face.

I couldn't focus—the pain was too great, my brain was desperate for oxygen, and I had no muscles left that could force my lungs to perform the task.

Stars. The thought somehow reached what little conscious thought I had left. I wanted to see my beloved stars one last time. Clouds were everywhere now. Just when I thought I might catch a glimpse of a star, Life would stand obstinately in the way.

I knew I only had moments left before my body shut down from the damage he had done. I wanted to scream but had no voice, much less oxygen, with which to propel it.

I wanted to push him out of the way so I could see my stars just one last time, but none of my muscles could respond. My entire body, with its complex system of nerves and sinews and muscle, was fighting a desperate battle to keep me alive. A battle I knew it was going to lose.

I strained to keep my eyes open in a desperate hope that somehow I could see them. Just a glimpse. One star would do, just one more time.

It wasn't to be. I watched helplessly as Life roared in anger and lifted his right foot, clearly aiming for the same spot his fists had pummeled on my chest. I couldn't even close my eyes as I watched the sole of his boot come crashing down to kill me.

I woke up in a cold sweat and sat straight up in bed. I was hyperventilating, and it took me half a second to realize where I was.

My home. My bedroom.

Alive!

Just like before. Just like it always was.

My mind registered the time on the nightstand: three o'clock in the morning.

So far, par for the course. I'd had a bad dream. I'd woken up in the middle of the night, but somehow I already knew this was different. And then it hit me.

The pain.

It wasn't nearly as bad as it had been in my dream, but it was there. A stabbing pain in my chest, left side. Not good.

I tried to rub it away, but it was still there.

Mary was sitting up. "What is it, honey?" she said. "Are you all right?"

I wanted to lie to her, to tell her everything was OK, but I knew this time it was different. "No," I said weakly, "I don't think so."

She was wide awake now. "What's wrong?"

"My chest hurts," I said finally, giving in to the inevitable. She was predictably upset. I wasn't exactly happy either.

The pain subsided, and we decided after a while that I didn't need to go to the hospital. We did, however, stay up the rest of the night talking. I finally told her about what was going on at work.

We spent the weekend discussing everything. About work, life, the book, our goals, our challenges. Every time the subject of work came up, I felt a pang in my chest. Even talking about an uncertain financial future if I were to leave my job didn't give me that pain in my chest. I would be scared, but it didn't give me pain. It was only when I thought about going to work on Monday, or even just talked about something to do with my job, that the pain returned. It wasn't as strong as it had been when I had woken up from my dream, but it was there.

"That's it!" Mary declared, seeing me rubbing my chest. "You're leaving!"

I wanted to argue with her. I wanted to explain to her how we couldn't afford to live on her salary alone. I wanted to tell her how I would just have to figure out how to deal with the stress. I wanted to find some reason why I couldn't leave, but the fact was, I knew she was right. If I didn't leave, there was a good possibility that the job would kill me just as surely as LIFE had done in my dream.

I went in on Monday morning and handed in my resignation.

Chapter 9
Arthur

Quitting a job with no immediate plan in place is an odd feeling.

The first sensation I felt was relief. As soon as I made the decision with Mary over the weekend, I knew it was the right one. Not that I didn't have reservations, because I did. I had a little money in my 401(k) and a bit in savings, but all of that would only get us by for eight months, maybe a year, if we were lucky. It was the immediate wave of relief that swept over me that told me I was making the right choice.

That, and the fact that the pain stopped. Instantly!

The next few weeks were interesting. My boss and coworkers were shocked, but of course life would go on for them, and I was simply one more employee moving through the grinding gears of the machine. I knew I'd miss some friends I'd made—well, more acquaintances than friends. Still, better that I should miss them than stay and end up in the hospital, or worse.

It took quite a bit of my time to transition my job to my temporary replacement, and I was working longer hours than ever just to get everything done.

My last day at work was surprisingly uneventful. My staff bought me a cake. There was a potluck lunch. I received some cards, a few hugs, and some handshakes, and then I walked out of the door for the last time as an employee. Surreal.

I wrote nonstop every day. I would meet with Violet as usual on Mondays, and we would go over any chapters I was working on. She would read what I had written the week before, making notes on pages that she would then hand back to me over lunch.

We went back through every chapter, making sure that I was doing the best I could. I wanted this book to really help people, and Violet understood it better than anyone. If something wasn't quite right, she would make me rework it—even if it meant starting over, which it did once or twice.

She prodded me when I was lagging, congratulated me when we got one chapter just right, and chastised me if she felt I wasn't trying hard enough. It was rough. She was not an easy taskmaster. I thought about telling her about my LIFE dreams at one point because they had stopped, but I figured the last person I would want knowing that about me was Violet. I hadn't even told Mary.

Our lunches no longer comprised awkward conversations. I was used to Violet's demeanor now, and when I arrived, I would hand over whatever work I had done since our last meeting, and she would start looking at it right away. I knew I could talk to her despite her being nose down in reading. She was, somehow, paying attention, but our lunches had become less about conversation and more about the book.

She would comment or answer my questions as she read, and I would take notes on my laptop. We would order food, of course, but it almost became a secondary purpose as we took over whatever table we were seated at with paper and laptop and scribbled notes.

As always, it only seemed to take Violet seconds to get to the heart of something that had taken me hours or days to write. Sometimes she challenged my logic to where I was almost certain it was flawed, only to find that she agreed with me but wanted me to think of all the potential scenarios.

She wasn't concerned with grammar or punctuation. Mary helped me with that when she could. Violet was focused exclusively on content. We reorganized chapters, moved sections around, and built the book like a jigsaw puzzle, until everything seemed to fit neatly and precisely together.

Four months after I left my job, I walked into the Denver Grill, guided as always by Gerald, and sat down in front of Violet with a big silly grin on my face.

She was in some sort of parachute-silk orange jumpsuit with yellow and red stripes, and her hair was once again fire-engine red. She must spend a fortune on hair products, I thought.

"Well," she said, "don't you look like the mouse who just ate the cheese?"

"I finished it," I said proudly, placing a flash drive on the table that contained my finished manuscript. Not that it wouldn't need professional editing, of course, but at least I had finished writing it.

Violet smiled at me. "Great," she said, meaning it. "How are you doing otherwise?"

For the first time, we talked not about my book or my old job, but about me and what I wanted to do next. The truth was, I wasn't sure. We spent our lunch hour going over various options, like going into consulting or some entrepreneurial venture. Even looking for a better job in my old field, but nothing felt quite right. Toward the end, we got back to the book.

"So," she said, "do you know what publishers you're going to send this to?"

"No," I said tentatively, "I don't know how all of that works and I'm kind of scared, to tell you the truth."

"Scared of what?"

"I don't know," I began. "I'm scared of the whole publishing world. I guess I just don't want to turn into one of those hucksters who hawk their wares at conventions."

Violet raised her eyebrow at me, which I realized was her way of encouraging me to go on.

"It's just that I've seen authors and speakers who get on a stage and tease the audience, giving them just enough to get them to buy their book or video or sign up for their services or what have you, but it doesn't seem right to me."

"Why not?" she asked, her eyes gazing past me to whatever caught her attention.

"Well," I said, "don't get me wrong, I know that's how the game is played, but I don't want to be someone who is just trying to sell books. I want to really help people." I was getting passionate again and my voice climbed. "I want to go out there and tell them everything. Everything that's in the book, everything I can think of that will help them start improving their lives. I don't want to give them a taste or a tease or somehow just get them interested. I want them to leave with actual tools, actual knowledge that will enable them to immediately start living a better life."

"And you don't think that's possible?"

"I don't know," I responded. "I don't think that's how publishers operate. They're in business to sell books. They're not concerned about helping the audience so much as they want to sell as many books as possible." I paused. "I don't know if what I want to do is even possible."

"Because . . ." she prodded.

"Because," I said, sighing, "my hope is that if I'm authentically giving everything I can, people will still buy the book. Maybe just to give to someone else, or to keep for themselves. It's not that I don't want to sell books, but I really want to be paid as a speaker to help people. I think if I can talk to people and explain the principles in this book, I can truly help them, and speaking to audiences is far more effective than one-on-one through the book. The problem is I'm not some big shot already-famous person. I'm not a doctor or a TV personality. I'm just me."

She paused, then leaned forward. "Maybe 'just me' is enough." She looked straight into my eyes and held my gaze for a moment or two before shifting her head to the right and scanning the room again.

I shook my head doubtfully.

"Just because something hasn't been done yet doesn't mean it can't be," Violet said, her eyes once again homing in on mine. "What questions could you be asking yourself instead of the ones that are keeping you from this goal?" Now she was grinning.

I had to laugh. Hearing my advice given back to me was something I wasn't used to. It also helped me understand just how hard it is to stay positive when things look negative. The next few months were going to show me just how hard it could be.

I began by looking online for publishers I thought my book might be of interest to. Then I went to the bookstore and wrote publisher's names and websites from some of the newer books in the self-help section. I even went to the library and got the most recent copy of The Writer's Market and went through it, making a list of potential publishers and literary agents to send my manuscript to.

Although the days of printing and mailing large manuscripts to publishers no longer existed thanks to the modern marvels of the internet and email, finding publishers was still no easy task. Once I had identified the ones I wanted to contact, they all had varying requirements for filling out their submission forms or sending emails. It took me a few weeks of searching and filling in online submission forms to get through the whole list.

It took several weeks before the first rejection arrived.

It came not in the form of a letter, as in days gone by, but as an impersonal email that looked just like a form letter would. "Thank you for your interest . . . not what we're looking for . . . best of luck to you . . ."

As the weeks went by, more rejections came. The publishers who at least seemed to have looked at what I had sent and taken the time to give me an honest assessment, offered one universal comment: No one liked the title.

Great, I thought. Not only does no one want to publish the book, but they hate the title as well.

I was also getting more than a little worried about the future. We had been living off Mary's salary, supplemented by my now liquidated 401(k). That had not been an easy task, either in concept or in execution. Everyone told me not to touch my 401(k). Even the company that managed it warned me on their website not to dip into it, and if I had to, they advised me not to use all of it.

The penalties and taxes were much higher than I thought, and what I actually ended up with was much less than I had hoped.

I had reasoned that either I would rebuild it when money was no longer a problem, or—and here is where I really reached deep for positive thinking—it occurred to me that I didn't simply want to work until retirement and then go out to pasture. I hoped to build something beyond me. Something that would go on helping people long after I was gone. A business that would allow me to live comfortably with Mary for the rest of our lives and perhaps leave a fund for a foundation after we were gone. Since we had no children of our own, perhaps it would be nice to support young people in the future to help them live better lives.

And so, I liquidated it all. No more safety net. No more security.

Time was going by too quickly. We were already almost halfway through the 401(k) money, and I hadn't earned a penny since I quit my job. I kept busy doing projects around the house, helping Mary with things for her job, and even putting together a loose skeleton of a website for myself for if and when someone actually wanted to publish my book.

Weeks passed, and I began researching the nebulous world of self-publishing. I had spent some time looking at hybrid publishers, a new breed of imprint publishers who would publish your book, but you had to commit to selling a certain quantity yourself. Many of them required that you buy those books, sometimes in the thousands, up front. That wasn't an option, not least of all because we didn't have the money, but primarily because I was determined not to be a traveling salesman trying to get people to buy my book.

Mary's contract had ended, and they hadn't renewed it. She had a few short consulting gigs, but the pay amounted to hundreds of dollars and we needed thousands. Time was running out.

I hadn't seen Violet in over a month. She was out of town and said she would be in touch.

One Thursday morning, I received a postcard in the mail from London. I saw her loopy handwriting with my name and address. The message on the card read simply:

July 18th. Lunch. Violet.

The eighteenth of July was the Monday after the following week.

I walked into the Denver Grill for the first time in almost two months. Gerald looked up when I walked in the door and seemed genuinely pleased to see me, saying, "Hello, Mr. Goodwin. Right this way, sir."

I followed him through the already bustling restaurant, looking toward the back, where Violet and I were usually seated, to see what she would be wearing today.

As we approached that part of the dining room, however, I couldn't find her. Not only was there no woman in vibrant colors sitting in a booth or at a table waiting for me, but I couldn't spot any seating that wasn't fully occupied, save one table where an older gentleman was sitting by himself.

I looked around, wondering if Gerald had forgotten which table Violet was sitting at, but I still couldn't see her anywhere. I turned back just in time; Gerald stopped at the table where the lone gentleman was sitting and said, "Here you are, sir."

I looked at Gerald questioningly, and then at the seated man. As Gerald left, I opened my mouth to protest when the man at the table stood up and held out his hand. "You must be Oliver Goodwin."

I turned to face him, looked at his hand, and slowly held out my own to shake it.

"Yes," I said, then, "I'm sorry. I was expecting someone else."

He smiled warmly as he sat back down and motioned to the seat across from him. "Yes, Violet asked me to meet with you."

Now I was really confused. "I'm sorry," I repeated. "Who exactly are you?"

"Forgive me," he said, holding his hand against his chest. "My name is Arthur Bennington."

Somewhere in his sixties, he was of medium height with a slim build and gray curly hair. His eyes were dark brown behind his round glasses. He was dressed in a gray suit with a light blue shirt and a blue diamond-patterned tie.

I felt underdressed in my slacks and simple button-down shirt.

"Why did Violet want you to meet me?" I asked, "And where is she?"

"Oh, I suspect she's still in England," he said, looking over his menu at me as he studied the daily chef's special. "As for why she wanted me to meet you? Because of your manuscript, of course."

"My manuscript?" I said slowly.

"She sent it to me."

I shook my head, trying to make sense of it all. "I don't understand," I said, putting my menu down on the table.

"She asked me to take a look at your manuscript," Arthur said, closing his menu and setting it aside. "I own PenBridge Publishing."

I didn't know what to say. I'd never heard of PenBridge Publishing before.

"Why did you write your book?" Arthur asked.

"Excuse me?" I said, caught off guard.

"What made you write your book? What were you hoping to accomplish?"

I sat back in my chair and thought about how best to answer him. Leaning forward and resting my forearms on the edge of the table, I decided to go with the truth. I said, "Because I want to help people."

He looked on saying nothing, so I continued, "I want people to know that anyone can have a better life, to get more out of life and not be burdened by the stress and pointless things we often focus on. I want to help people spend their lives doing the important things, not the mundane ones. To remember what it was like to be a child and dream and to follow those dreams."

I paused and looked over Arthur's shoulder, not really focusing on anything as I remembered my own dreams. I said, "I want to help people understand that life is meant to be lived, not endured."

"Yes," he said, his voice gentle and low, "that was something you said in the book. It makes a great quote."

I raised my eyebrows in surprise. He'd actually read the whole book. That line was near the end of the manuscript.

"What are your publishing goals?" He leaned back, one hand on top of the other, as he looked at me through his round glasses.

Publishing goals? I had no idea what my publishing goals were. I didn't even know one had publishing goals as an author. "I don't understand," I said simply.

I don't remember what I ate. Arthur asked questions, and I did my best to answer them. He was easy to talk to and not at all what I pictured a publisher would look like, much less act like. At one point, he asked me if I wanted to use the book as a platform to speak.

I told him my fear of being a "traveling book salesman," and he laughed, his smile widening as I described my notion of truly helping people, not just selling books. "I'm sure that's not what you want to hear as a publisher, but I don't want to lie to you," I said. "It's not that I don't want to sell books, I do, but only from the standpoint that I truly believe the book can help people, not because I want to make a lot of money selling books."

"How do you expect to earn a living?"

I pursed my lips and half smiled. "I haven't quite figured that out yet."

He nodded, as if contemplating my answer, then asked me more about my ideas on speaking and what I hoped the book would do. Finally, as the lunch crowd was thinning out, he looked across the table at me and said, "Oliver, I'd like to publish your book."

I must have looked silly because I just sat there dumbfounded.

Arthur continued, "You are just the author I've been looking for, and I think your book is terrific. You really have something special there, and I'd be honored to publish it."

"Really?" was all I could manage to say. I couldn't believe someone finally wanted to publish my book.

"Yes, really." Arthur smiled. "PenBridge isn't a large publishing house, but we're pretty good at what we do. You're exactly the kind of author I want to be associated with, and together I think we can get your book out and really help people."

"Um, that's great!" I managed to say, a huge grin on my face. "How does this work?" Then I added honestly, "I really don't have any idea about this, being a first-time author."

He nodded. "I understand." Then, removing his glasses to clean them with his napkin, he said, "I'll send you our standard contract tonight by email. Look it over, and if you have any questions, just let me know." Then he added, "If you're OK with the contract, I'll get in touch with an editor to have them work on the fine tuning."

He put up his hand slightly as if warning me and said, "Don't worry, we're not going to change much. I like what you've written. Editors help make it flow better."

He needn't have worried; I was fully expecting someone to look at the editing. I was a lousy speller, even with spellcheck, and even though both Mary and Violet had caught errors, I was sure there were more. My grammar was even worse. I smiled. "I have no problem with an editor, Arthur, and I can use all the help I can get."

"Good, good," he said, then added hesitantly, "There's just one thing."

I beat him to it. "You don't like the title."

"Well," he started, a thin grin tugging at the corners of his mouth, "I think we could perhaps improve it. We want something that grabs people."

I sighed. "OK."

We talked through several ideas but eventually agreed that we'd mull it over and email each other if we had any other thoughts.

Despite that last bit of disappointing news, I left feeling like I was ten feet tall. I couldn't wait to get home and tell Mary.

Chapter 10
Holly

The next day, I received an email from Arthur with an attached contract. I read through it and was pleasantly surprised. Although PenBridge didn't pay advances (which I had learned were a thing of the past, unless you were someone famous or a former president), their royalty payments were more than fair. Best of all, it wouldn't cost me anything to get the book published. PenBridge would publish the book, get it online on all the major sites, and make it available through two large distributors that I had actually heard of.

Mary was jumping up and down. "Oliver, you actually have a publishing contract!"

I smiled at her and, as usual, my realistic nature was a little more subdued. "Yes," I agreed, "but we're going to have to do a lot of work ourselves. They don't do book tours or anything these days, so we're going to have to figure out how to get the book out there."

Mary would not let anything like logic get in the way of her excitement. She insisted we go out to celebrate, and she told everyone from the server to the couple sitting next to us that I was a published author. I suppose there are worse things your wife can embarrass you with.

Arthur and I kept in touch through email. I worked through the cover design with him and the editing with someone named Joe, whom I emailed back and forth with as we worked to "get the book as tight as we could"—his words, not mine.

One day, I received a call from Arthur. "Hello, Oliver," he said, "I just got the final layout from Joe, so we're just about ready to put it to print once we figure out the title."

I told him how excited I was. "Yes, I'll bet," he said in his warm, friendly way. "Listen, we'll send you ten copies on us once it prints, but I wondered if you'd like to order extra copies. You know, to give out to friends and have with you for speaking and such."

I told him I was still fairly new to all this and wasn't sure how many I would need. I was afraid to tell him I did not know what I was doing now that I had finished writing, and I was apprehensive about how I was going to speak to audiences about it. Of course, what frightened me even more was that I had no idea how to get in front of audiences in the first place.

We talked for a little while about what authors typically start with and ended up with a number I could live with, financially speaking. We batted around a few more ideas for the title and still couldn't find something we both felt good about. We laughed jovially, and I rang off with mixed feeling of excitement and foreboding.

I hadn't seen Violet in weeks, and when I sent her an email asking if she'd like to have lunch, there was no reply.

A few days later, I received a telephone call from a woman who said her name was Holly and that she worked with Arthur at PenBridge. She said she was going to be in

Denver the following week and wanted to meet with me to discuss marketing for my book.

We met at a coffee shop downtown. It was one of those local Boulder coffee shops that had expanded into Denver. It was the type of place that spends little on decor, with mismatched tables and odds and ends for decoration. It was also the type that has young baristas who look like ski bums, but who serve excellent coffee and know by name the locals who stop in.

I, of course, wasn't one of those locals and neither was Holly, so it was easy to pick out the one person who looked a little out of place. She was younger than me, probably in her late twenties. She had jet-black hair down to her shoulders, brown eyes, and a warm smile. She stood and shook my hand, and after I grabbed some coffee, I sat down at her table.

She told me she was Arthur's niece. She lived in Austin, Texas, but she had helped do some things for PenBridge ever since Arthur's wife passed away a little over a year ago.

Mostly, it seemed, she dealt with the financial end of things at the publishing company, but she also helped work on marketing, as that was her professional background outside of her uncle's business.

"The first thing we have to do," Holly said, getting down to business, "is figure out the title for your book."

I stifled a groan and tried to keep an open mind. I flashed back to a conversation with Mary that had followed my bemoaning the fact that even my publisher didn't like my title.

"Oliver," she had said sweetly—almost too sweetly. "I know it's difficult for you, but it sounds like this is a common theme from the publishers you've heard from." She waited to see if I was going to react, and when I didn't, she continued. "They obviously know what works and what doesn't, and just because you can't have the title you want doesn't mean you can't use it in the book. Just try to keep an open mind and see what they have to say."

I had agreed, but of course it was much easier to agree with Mary than it was to sit down across the table from Holly and admit that my book didn't have a good title. Holly tried to make it easier for me.

"It's not that we hate your title, Mr.…."—she caught herself, as we had already determined she should call me Oliver and I would call her Holly—"… Oliver. It's just that we don't think people will understand it."

I couldn't help myself. "But that's the whole point," I said pleadingly. "It catches your attention, and the book explains what it's all about."

She nodded, and for a moment I thought I might be winning her over. Then she said, "I see what you're saying, but in today's day and age, information is coming at people much faster than they have time for. If a blog is more than two or three paragraphs long, most people won't even read it. We need to give them a title that they can understand and get excited about, not one they have to think about. Too many of them won't spend the time to give thought to what it's about, much less pick it up to find out."

So much for winning her over.

"I have to confess," she said, "that I have not yet read the book."

I murmured something about my not having expected her to, though the truth was, I was a little disappointed. Of course, it was ridiculous of me to expect everyone at PenBridge to have read my book.

"Can you tell me what it's about so I can help you find a title that will . . ."—I was sure she was searching for the right phrasing that wouldn't offend me—"… grab people's attention and speak to them?"

Swallowing what little was left of my pride and acknowledging that I was going to have to give up the title I thought was so clever, I began telling her about the book.

She asked great questions, and soon we were both talking back and forth, throwing out ideas and titles like confetti.

We had several possibilities, but none of them felt right. I couldn't quite put my finger on why, and even Holly agreed that our list didn't have the "perfect" title for a book that she said sounded "incredibly powerful."

"Tell me more about why you wanted to write the book and what you hope to accomplish by writing it," she said.

I began explaining something similar to what I had told Arthur when suddenly she interrupted me. "That's it!"

"What?" I asked, still processing what was left of the point I had been making.

"The title," she said, a gleam in her dark brown eyes. I waited.

"You've been talking about it this whole time—I just didn't pick up on it earlier until you started telling me why you wanted to write the book." Then she added, "You must have said something like it at least half a dozen times when we were discussing what the book was about." She smiled. "It's why you wrote it and it's what you want it to do for people."

Her smile widened. "Your title should be A Better Life."

She waited as I took in the idea before adding, "That's really what you want to help people do—live a better life—isn't it?" I started nodding. It was perfect. It was exactly what I wanted to do, and the title was simple, short, and grabbed you. Brilliant.

The book arrived without fanfare one day. I answered a knock at the door to find a box that the retreating UPS man had dropped off. I checked who it was addressed to as I picked it up. The weight of the box surprised me, as it wasn't all that big, but when I saw the printed address label from PenBridge, I caught my breath.

I took the box inside and opened it slowly. There, staring back at me, were ten copies of the book with my name in bold at the bottom. Mary was over the moon with excitement, and she took more than a few pictures of me holding it so she could blast the news to her social media friends.

I realized I had been holding my breath. I let it out slowly, letting the butterflies in my stomach calm down as the breath left me and after I got over the surrealness of seeing my name on the cover of a book, I began to get my hopes up as well. We talked about how we could market it online and set up some signings with local bookstores. We even discussed what a book tour might look like. I climbed into bed that night with a smile on my face, but as I turned off my bedside light and lay down, I felt the tiniest twinge of doubt creeping in.

That night I had a return visit from my old friend, LIFE. I spent the better part of my dreams trying to find my way out of a maze. Instead of dead ends, however, I would turn a corner and catch a glimpse of his red boxing glove as it came crashing down on my head or landed gut-wrenchingly in my stomach. I never found the way out. I woke up sore, tired, and with a feeling of dread. I had no idea what my endless turns and trials through the maze meant, but whatever it was, I knew I wasn't going to like it.

Chapter 11
Reality Check

Writing a book, it seemed, was no longer the novelty it had once been. Anyone could write a book these days, and with the various self-publishing options available and the advances in technology, there was no shortage of new ones. In fact, there seemed to be more books being published every day than there were people to read them.

PenBridge was not a large publishing house, and I was not a well-known, best-selling author. Although Arthur and Holly had done an amazing job of putting together and printing my book, marketing was up to me. Holly had helped me secure a few internet radio interviews, in which I had nervously taken part. Although Mary's vast online network of friends had said they would order a copy of my book, the truth was not many people knew it even existed, much less went out and bought a copy. My goal of starting a movement to help people live better lives was fading.

To make matters worse, Mary lost one of her last big contracts because of some sort of grant funding mix-up, and the company had been forced to reshuffle priorities. Although she still had one or two smaller clients, we were now living largely off what was left of the 401(k), which was rapidly dwindling. I looked ahead and realized that in the not-too-distant future, that money was going to run out, and with it, any means of income we had.

I started looking online at job postings; each time I did, I felt my stomach lurch and unfailingly had restless nights fighting with LIFE. Still, I dreaded what might happen to our home, our lifestyle—indeed, our lives—if I didn't somehow earn an income and soon.

Mary noticed my restless nights again. We sat around the kitchen table one Saturday morning as I discussed the desperate situation that I felt lay ahead of us financially.

I could tell I was worrying her, but I saw no way around it. Hiding fears from each other just wasn't the way we lived.

"What about your speaking plans?" she asked me at one point.

"Well," I lamented, "I've been trying to find ways of getting myself out there, but I have had little luck. I've filled out dozens of 'call for speaker' applications online, but a lot of them want you to speak for free."

"That might not be a bad thing at first," Mary said. "At least it would get your name out there."

"True," I replied, "but we don't have that much time." I threw my hands up. "I can't afford to speak for free and hope that it eventually leads to paying gigs. We will be homeless by the time that happens."

"No, we won't," she said, but I could sense the doubt creeping into her as well.

We spent the next few weeks trying to market my book and promote my availability as a speaker across the internet and social media. Mary contacted Arthur and Holly and started brainstorming ideas with them. While many friends voiced their support and encouragement, no engagements were forthcoming.

One evening over dinner, I said perhaps we should reach out to Arthur and Holly and see if they had any more ideas. Mary paused a little too long before answering, and I said, "What's wrong?"

"Oh, nothing," she mumbled.

"What is it?" I asked, knowing there was something she wasn't telling me.

She was hesitant, but after a few moments she said, "I don't know, it's just a feeling I have."

"What feeling?"

"Just some things Holly said the last couple of times I talked to her." She paused before continuing. "I don't want to worry you, but I get the feeling that PenBridge hasn't been doing too well financially."

We talked about how her conversations with Holly had gone, and I had to admit, it certainly didn't sound positive. Although she hadn't come out and said it, the gist had been that she was helping her uncle because business had been slowly worsening in the publishing industry. Small publishing firms like PenBridge were either going out of business or being gobbled up by the larger publishing houses, though that was rare. No one was knocking on PenBridge's doors to buy them. Holly had been going through the business aspects of her uncle's company over the last few months and wasn't sure how much longer it could survive.

I spent the evening up in my office, wracking my brain for what to do next. Mary had been right in not wanting to tell me. Now, not only was I worried about our own future but that of Arthur and his business as well. Holly, although divorced from her ex-husband, was still young and had a promising career if PenBridge was to go under. For Arthur, this was his life's work. He had believed in me and taken a chance on me, and now I was letting him down, too.

I spent that night in what felt like a fight to the death with LIFE. When I woke up the next morning, I wasn't sure if it was a blessing or a curse.

I walked into the Denver Grill two days later after Violet got back to me, having slept for only a few hours in three days and looking every bit as bad as I felt. Gerald said nothing, but his raised eyebrow upon seeing me spoke volumes.

Violet showed no emotion as I sat down wearily opposite her, but her words were straight and to the point: "You look terrible."

"Thanks," I said sarcastically.

"What's happened?" she asked. "I thought the book came out looking great?"

"Yeah, it looks great, but no one even knows it exists."

Her head swiveled about the room in her familiar fashion as we talked. "What do you mean?" she asked.

I told her about my attempts to market the book online and how miserable the success rate had been. I told her about my even less successful attempts at becoming a speaker. As the words left my mouth, even I could hear the whining in my voice, and I felt even more depressed for complaining about my problems to her.

"So now what?" she asked bluntly.

I sighed heavily, and with my elbows on the table, I put my face in my hands. "I have no idea."

Her reply caused me to lift my head sharply. "Guess you might as well give up then."

"What?" I asked incredulously.

"Well," she said, "it looks to me like you've given up, and it certainly sounds like you have, so why don't you?"

"I didn't say I was giving up," I shot back.

"Sure looks like it to me," she said matter-of-factly, looking around the room as if I wasn't even there.

I was still amazed, after all this time, at how quickly she could get under my skin. "I'm not giving up." I said, like a petulant child who doesn't like what they've been told. "I'm just not sure what to do next."

She swiveled her head back to me, and her deep blue eyes bored into mine as she spoke. "What did you think would happen? Did you think you would write your book and the masses would suddenly wake up and jump out of bed to go and read it?"

She didn't give me any time to reply before saying, "Did you think it was going to be easy?"

I opened my mouth to reply, but she cut me off. "Do you think authors are special and don't have to work hard to be successful?"

"No," I began, "of course not, I just . . ."

"You just what?" she interrupted. "You thought writing the book would be the hard part?"

I still hated the fact that she seemed to read my mind sometimes.

When I paused, not knowing how to answer, she went on, "You of all people should know that this was never going to be easy. Yes, your book can change people's lives, and yes, it's something that everyone needs, but just because eating more fruits and vegetables is good for you doesn't mean people do it."

Her gaze hadn't wavered from my eyes, and I felt the full weight of her intensity on me as she continued, "How can you expect to help people and change their lives when you won't even change your own?"

"What?" I growled, taking offense at her last comment.

She simply raised her eyebrows and responded, "What, you think you've been asking the right questions lately? You think you've been living a 'better life' since your book came out? Look at you!" she cocked her head in mock disgust.

I was speechless. Partly because my sense of pride was hurt, and I was shocked at the way she was talking to me, but mostly because, deep down, I knew she was right. I sat for a moment staring at her and finally looked away in shame. "You're right," was all I could say.

Silence stretched between us as I looked down at the table, embarrassed and ashamed. Her voice broke the silence. While it wasn't exactly warm and consoling, it no longer held the heat it had moments ago.

"So again, I'll ask you. Now what?"

I tried to summon up some emotion—courage, or passion, or something—to answer her question, but I was simply too tired. And so I said softly and with little enthusiasm, "I need to start asking better questions."

"Yes," she said, loudly enough for me to look up at her. "You do!"

Violet's eyes seemed to shine with a brightness I couldn't quite describe, and her intense gaze, as she leaned forward toward me to catch my own, sent a small shiver down my spine. As intensely as they were illuminated, her eyes suddenly seemed to soften, and she cocked her head slightly to one side as she continued. "Nothing worthwhile is ever easy, Oliver." Her voice, too, had softened and become more gentle. "And I can think of nothing as worthwhile as your purpose in writing your book and what you want to do for the people who read it."

I knew acutely that for the last several moments, her gaze had not left my face. Her propensity for shifting her attention around the room was absent, and I knew that whatever was happening between us at that moment was pivotal.

"No one said it would be easy," she continued. "In fact, if it was easy, it wouldn't be as important as the movement you are creating." She paused to let her words sink into my mind and then continued, "But hard isn't the problem.

You've done hard things before. The problem you have is that you don't believe in yourself."

Ouch, that one hurt even more than the rest.

She wasn't about to let me feel sorry for myself, though. "You need to figure out how to change that, Oliver. Plenty of people believe in you, and if you can't believe in yourself, then you're not only wasting your life, but you're wasting the time and energy those people have put into you."

People at the surrounding tables were beginning to notice the intensity of the conversation, not to mention the loudness of Violet's voice, which was climbing again. I wanted to look away, to walk away even, but I knew that was impossible. I couldn't take my eyes off the bright blue of hers. "This is much bigger than you, Oliver. Only you can do this work, and it's up to you to do it!"

Suddenly, she sat back in her seat and looked left and right, her gaze quickly causing those sitting on either side who had been looking at us to avert their eyes. She fixed her gaze once more upon me. "Don't you dare give up! Keep going, whatever it takes. Start asking different questions. Start finding different answers. Your success will not come from finding the perfect way or because someone suddenly discovers you. Your success will come from perseverance."

And just as quickly as it began, her reprimand was over. She picked up the menu and began talking about what to eat for lunch.

I decided that although I would not ask Arthur about his business affairs, if his success did indeed depend on my own, at least I should involve him in my plans. So, I called him that afternoon, and we began discussing various strategies and ideas for getting my book out in front of people.

I asked him if he knew of any way I could get myself out there as a speaker. I reiterated that I felt the best way I could help people was by speaking to them in groups rather than one-on-one through the book.

He said it made sense. If I was as passionate in front of audiences as I was with him, it was likely that more people would want to buy the book after hearing me speak. I knew that was the publisher in him talking, and even though I didn't disagree with what he was saying, I was less worried about selling books than I was about helping people.

My mind wanted to revolt at that thought, since selling books was how I had chosen to make a living. My home, my family, and even Arthur's business looked like it depended on my success in doing so. Still, I couldn't shake the notion that my plan felt right. It felt more authentic, more me. I wanted to focus on helping people, not on being a peddler of something.

The more I thought about it, the more I became impassioned about the idea. It just made sense. As I reflected that night upon my life, I realized that despite my worries about my finances, I was happier than I had ever been. Living at home and being able to spend more time with Mary, to write at my own schedule, to enjoy the home that Mary and I had built—it was the best I had felt in years. Even spending more time with Marlow seemed to make both of our lives better.

I realized that regardless of what happened in the future, this was what life was all about. It was never about the things or the career—life was about the experiences and the people that mattered. Somehow, some way, I would figure out the future, but what good would the future be if I couldn't enjoy the present?

Mary, as if sensing some change in me, even came to bed that night with a renewed sense of optimism. She told me how proud she was of all that I had done, and how she believed in me and "us."

"I'm not sure how it's all going to work out, Oliver," she said, "but I believe in you and I believe in that book of yours. I just know better things are coming, and you are going to be every bit the man you wanted to be when you wrote it."

For the first time in a long while, I slept peacefully through the night.

The next morning, I found a letter taped to my laptop. It was from Mary.

My Darling Oliver,

I know you're worried, and I can't explain why, but I'm not.

I believe in you so much and I know how incredible your book and your work is. I believe in what you're doing, I believe in what you have done with your book, and I believe in you.

Don't give up. Don't give in. Keep moving forward, one step at a time.

You are the most incredible man I know, and I have no doubt that you're going to help a lot of people with what you're doing.

Hang in there. I love you.
Your Mary.

With support like that, it was much easier to avoid giving up.

Arthur called a few weeks later.

"Oliver," he said happily, "what are you doing the first week in October?"

As we were already in September, I didn't have to think too far ahead. "Nothing, why?"

"Well," he said, sounding pleased with himself, "I got you a speaking engagement."

"Really?" I said, smiling.

"They won't pay a lot," he said, mentioning a small sum, but at least they were willing to pay me. "It's a convention in San Diego, and they're willing to pay your airfare as well."

I didn't know what to say. An out-of-state speaking engagement paid, and they would fly me out there. It was almost too good to be true.

"They won't pay for a hotel, so you might have to fly out and back in the same day unless you want to pay for one yourself," Arthur said.

I told him flying out and back wouldn't be a problem. He mentioned I'd be able to have books at the convention bookstore and that he and Holly would take care of it.

I thanked him profusely and hung up, feeling excited and nervous at the same time. Up to this point, I had spoken only a few times about my book. A friend of Mary's, who was a professor at a local community college, had generously invited me to speak frequently to a small group of college students. Speaking at a convention was a different matter. I'd likely be in a hotel ballroom in front of dozens or maybe a few hundred people.

I spent the next few weeks working on a presentation, trying to make sure I could impart as many of the tools from my book as possible in the time I was allotted. Arthur said he thought I would have between forty-five and ninety minutes. I planned for forty-five, as I knew talking more would be easier than talking less.

Mary was predictably excited when I told her. She not only helped me work on my presentation but also let me practice on her and Marlow. Marlow seemed less impressed, often going to the corner of the room to circle a few times before lying down in the middle of my talk.

Mary, on the other hand, was good at giving me constructive feedback, but she also said that she thought my talk was "exceptional." I tried to believe her, even though my own lack of confidence and my logically oriented brain said that, of course, she would say that. She was my wife.

The only thing that upset Mary was that a client had insisted she be in New York that week, so she wouldn't be able to go with me. We both knew that we needed the money; telling the client no just wasn't an option. I told her it was probably just as well, as I would be nervous enough as it was and didn't need the added pressure of having my wife in the audience.

"Oh well," she said, "I'm sure there will be plenty of other chances for me to hear you speak."

I stifled the worry and doubt that always tried to rear its head whenever she talked like that. Instead, I focused on asking better questions.

While we were going to bed one night, Mary put down her iPad and gazed intently over at me through her glasses. I looked into her big brown eyes as she said, "I do believe in you, you know."

I smiled back and replied, "I know," but she leaned over, took my hand in hers, and waited until she was sure she had my full attention.

"What you're doing is important," she said. "More important than I think you realize." I smiled weakly, about to reply, but she squeezed my hand and continued, "I mean it, Oliver. What you wrote in that book—the principles you teach and the way you want to help people—is something people need. I am so proud of you."

I felt myself getting emotional, and I swallowed hard.

"I know you're going to be terrific at the conference," she said, "and even if you don't feel like you will, know that I am certain of it." She paused. "Use my belief in you if you have to, because eventually, you will know I'm right."

She leaned forward and gave me a long goodnight kiss. Mary had always been my biggest champion. Not for the first time, I felt her love deep inside of me and knew just how truly lucky I was that this incredible woman chose me.

I lay down and stared out the window at the stars, willing her faith in me to spread itself into my own belief.

The day of the conference was rapidly approaching, and I needed all the help I could get.

Chapter 12
All or Nothing

I flew out at the crack of dawn and landed in San Diego just before ten o'clock. Holly had sent a text while I was in flight, telling me where to meet her. Since I hadn't brought any checked luggage, I soon climbed into a hired Lincoln Town Car next to her just outside Lindbergh Field Airport.

She asked how my flight had been, and I replied with a nervous smile that it had been fine. The temperatures were warm yet humid. I looked out the window at the bright sunshine and the palm trees that flashed by as we headed away from the rest of the airport traffic.

I remembered having read somewhere that just next to the runways was one of the Marine boot camp bases, and not far away was where Navy SEALs did their infamous BUDS training on Coronado Island. I could have used some of the confidence of the SEALs who had finished their training.

These trivial bits of information kept my mind occupied for all of two minutes. Soon enough, we were passing the typical slate of hotels near every airport. My mind instantly came back to reality and with it, the adrenaline rush of fear.

Holly did her best to distract me with information about the convention and the name of the person she had been working with. I was scheduled to speak at two o'clock in the afternoon, which would give me a little time to prepare.

More like a little time to get even more nervous, I thought, but I decided not to say that out loud.

We arrived at the hotel just before eleven and quickly made our way toward the conference center of the mammoth building. As we were walking by the main amphitheater that the hotel chain had built to rival the various stadiums in the area, one door opened. I looked just in time to give my heart a little more adrenaline, as if it needed it. What I saw looked just like a stadium where you might watch a sporting event or a concert. There were at least two sections of seats rising from the floor, and as far as my quick glance could see, almost every seat was taken.

I cleared my throat, trying not to sound as nervous as I felt. "Holly, how many people are attending this conference?"

Without missing a beat, she said, "Oh, somewhere around five or ten thousand, I think," as if it was normal.

I stopped walking in the middle of the hallway. It took her a few steps before she realized I was no longer at her side. She turned around and saw me standing with my mouth open in shock. She smiled, walked back to me, and took my arm, urging me forward. "It's OK," she giggled, "it doesn't matter if you're talking to ten people or ten thousand. Just find someone near the front and have a conversation with them." She made it sound so easy. "You'll be fine," she added as we approached the door at the back of the stage.

Famous last words.

We entered a corridor that led behind the stage. Soon, we found ourselves in a large ready area where throngs of people were walking around with headsets on, talking or mumbling, seemingly to themselves. It was all hectic, and

Holly kept asking them one by one for someone named Meagan. Following the pointing gestures of the backstage crew, we ended up standing next to a tall, blond woman in a blue suit and skirt and a frilly white shirt. She was wearing one of the headsets, talking earnestly while tapping a pen loudly against the paper on her clipboard.

"Yes, yes, I know, but we'll have to figure out a way to get the presentation in the slide deck before they go on." She listened to the reply and then said rather forcefully, "I don't care what Nick says. I'm telling you to do it, so get it done."

She turned toward us as if she were going somewhere in a hurry. "Oh," she said when she saw us, unaware that we had been standing there.

Holly put out her hand. "Hi, Meagan?" she asked, then said, "I'm Holly Bennington-Horne, from PenBridge Publishing. We spoke on the phone."

Meagan stared blankly back for a brief second until recognition caught up with her. "Oh, right, great," she said, and shook Holly's hand.

Holly half turned and said, "This is Oliver Goodwin."

"Oh, thank God you're here!" Meagan blurted, with more relief than I thought necessary since I was three hours early.

Little did I know.

By way of explanation, Meagan said, "We've had to change a few things. You're now at eleven twenty. You'll have fifteen minutes." And she brushed by me, suddenly in a hurry and looking back over her shoulder. "You don't need a presentation, do you? You know, PowerPoint, Prezi, or something? I don't think we'll have time to get it on the projector."

"What?" Holly exclaimed, voicing the surprise I was too dumbfounded to express. "Stay here!" she commanded before striding off after Meagan, her heels clicking loudly on the floor as she began voicing her protests.

I looked around, not knowing quite what to do. There were some double doors to my left; a white sign permanently mounted to one of them said "Quiet! Backstage." I definitely wasn't going in there. People were coming and going around me. Not knowing where I was supposed to be, and still reeling from the impossible notion that I was supposed to go on stage in twenty minutes—and present what was supposed to last nearly an hour, in only fifteen minutes—wasn't leaving me with a clear head.

Not wanting to stand still, I followed the path Holly had taken.

I passed a few more doors, each with a forbidding sign on it, and just as I was about to give up and head back to where I had been told to wait, I heard Holly's voice. She was still clearly angry.

"You can't do this. It's not fair," I heard her say as I trudged toward the sound of her voice. I came around the corner at the end of the hall and found a single door propped open, which was labeled "Green Room." Peering around the doorway, I saw Holly and Meagan, and another woman standing with them.

I knew who she was. This was her event, and she was the one responsible for the entire showcase. I'd seen her picture on the information we had received while checking in at registration a few minutes ago. She had shoulder-length dark hair and long eyelashes, was of average height, though made taller by the high-heeled shoes she was wearing. She wore a floor-length blue-and-white beaded ball gown with diamond teardrop earrings. I was sure that her large, sparkling necklace, which was full of jewels and diamonds, cost more than my car.

Meagan stood with a cell phone in her hand, reaching out to the woman in charge. Holly was standing rigidly with her fists balled and her shoulder halfway in between the two women.

The dark-haired woman turned and looked straight at Holly. She seemed to size her up, and her conclusion was not flattering. "Listen, honey," she said condescendingly, "the only reason your . . ."

She trailed off, looking over at Meagan, who said, "Oliver Goodwin," after looking at the clipboard in her hands.

"The only reason Mr. Goodwin is here at all is because my father knew your uncle. I was just doing him a favor. If you don't want the fifteen minutes, I'm sure we can get someone else to fill it." And with that, she took the phone from Meagan's hand, said, "Yes Jerry, what is it now?" and walked deeper into the greenroom and out of my sight.

Holly was fuming. Her fists were clenching and unclenching, and her breathing was coming in shallow, rapid gasps. Meagan followed her boss, leaving Holly alone in the small space. She turned, clearly intent on storming out of the room, but she stopped suddenly when she saw me. "How long . . ." she began.

I swallowed. "Long enough."

All the anger seemed to leave her body. She looked at me with genuine concern in her eyes as she approached. "Oliver, I'm so sorry," she said, then added, "Look, let's just go. You don't have to do this. I'll call my uncle. I'm sure he'll have a few choice words to say with Ms. . . ."

I put my arms out and grabbed her shoulders. "No," I said gently but firmly. "Arthur went to a lot of trouble to arrange this, and now that we're here, we will not let him down."

"But fifteen minutes!" she protested. "You can't cover your book in fifteen minutes."

She was right, of course, which is why what came out of my mouth next surprised me more than her. "I know. So, I won't try."

She looked at me with her big brown eyes, confused. "But then, what will you talk about?"

"I don't know," I said honestly. "I'll figure something out. Why don't you find out where I'm supposed to be while I think?"

I really had no idea what I was saying, and as Holly began walking back the way we had come, I felt very alone. I didn't want to go in the greenroom. I was unsure if this was the only entrance and didn't want to run into the dragon lady and her sidekick, so I just paced back and forth in the hallway. I looked at my watch. Ten minutes after eleven.

Ten thousand people. Fifteen minutes.

There was no way I was going to get through this. What Arthur had hoped for, and what I had readily gone along with to save both his business and my home, would be all for nothing if I failed.

Perhaps it was desperation or simply because I was too frightened to think, but the image of Violet suddenly flashed through my mind. What would she do if she were here? She would ask one of her inane and annoying questions. Something like "What if you could give an amazing presentation in fifteen minutes? What would that be?"

I stopped pacing.

I heard nothing Holly said when she came back to get me. I just followed blindly as she led me through the maze of hallways to the backstage entrance. She kept looking at me worriedly. I knew she was asking if I was OK. Doubtless, I must have repeatedly said yes, though I couldn't swear to it.

Suddenly, we were in the dark area backstage. There, a woman dressed all in black clipped a wireless microphone pack to the back of my belt, ran the lavaliere mic up through my shirt, and clipped it to the front. She told me to say "Mic check one two," which I did. She listened to her headset and nodded confidently. And then I was climbing a small set of stairs off to the side of the main stage. A man also dressed in black, with "Floor Director" emblazoned on his back like he was a member of some police SWAT unit, told me to wait as I reached the top of the last step.

I could see the audience clapping for the last speaker, who was heading toward the other end of the stage where another man in black awaited him. Although I could hear clapping, it seemed almost like background noise against the hollow sound of my own heartbeat that rang in my head. The conference emcee, a tall, good-looking Latino man with slicked-back black hair and a matching suit, walked to the center of the stage where a glass podium stood. "Wasn't that terrific?" he said jovially, sending the audience into another round of applause.

My stomach was churning. I could feel pangs of doubt creeping up. I was sweating a little and my heart was racing. As I looked around the coliseum at the massive audience, I swallowed loudly, at least to my ears, and wondered just how crazy I must be.

"OK, folks," the emcee said as the audience calmed down. "I know you're all ready for the lunch break and it's coming, I promise you, but before you head out for food, we have one more quick speaker for you. I promise he'll be brief."

A part of my mind wanted to protest, *Great, I'm the guy keeping everyone from their lunch*, but I was too wound up now. My heart was racing. My mind was spinning, and my breath was coming in quick, short bursts. This was it. The emcee was telling them about the book and winding down his introduction.

"So help me welcome to the stage"—he glanced at his notes—"Oliver Goodwin."

My last thought as I pounded my right fist into the palm of my left hand and literally ran onto the stage was, *At least he got my name right*.

Chapter 13
Fifteen Minutes

I surprised the emcee by heading straight toward him as he turned to leave. He half recoiled as I reached him. I quickly shook his hand and continued past him to the front of the stage. The audience was clapping respectfully; it was obvious they had never heard of me.

"Thank you," I said enthusiastically. "Thank you very much."

I took a deep breath, and for the second time in a year, I jumped headlong off the edge of a cliff.

The polite applause stopped and everything got eerily quiet. "I wrote a book about questions. About how questions can empower every area of your life," I said. I was talking fast, not only out of nerves, but because I had so little time. I wanted to make sure they could understand me, but I also needed to get through so many concepts. Plus, talking fast helped keep me excited, and I hoped it would come across to the audience as passionate.

"I was supposed to talk to you this afternoon, and I had hoped to tell you everything that was in the book. Give you all the tools, all the secrets, everything, so that you would leave here and be able to implement them *immediately*!" I shouted the last word to emphasize the point.

I could only see the part of the audience that was near the front. The stage lights were blinding, and a spotlight was shining directly into my eyes. Still, I could see that at least there was curiosity in some faces. I snuck a quick backward glance to the side of the stage and saw both the emcee and Meagan standing there. They were looking on with worried expressions.

"But then the organizers of this incredible event came to me and said they needed to rearrange the lineup, and they asked me if there was any way I could help them. They wondered if I could switch my time slot, and instead of what I had originally planned, they wanted me to give you something better. Something even more powerful and more impactful than my original presentation, and they wanted me to do it in *fifteen minutes*." Again, I emphasized the last two words.

I let that sink in for just a second as I glanced once again to the side of the stage. I saw Meagan and the emcee look at each other with even more worried expressions, and then I turned back to the audience. "I said, 'Absolutely, I have *just the thing*!'" I smiled the biggest smile I could. I was still scared, but now I was committed. I saw a few of the people in the front, smiling back. "*So*," I shouted again, almost causing the microphone to "feedback" into the speakers, "*are you ready?*"

The audience was intrigued, and I heard a few voices cry out, "Yeahhh!"

"OK," I said, striding across the stage to get my momentum going, "get out your notebooks because *here we go!*"

I could feel my heart racing, and while some of it was definitely nerves, I also knew that I was connecting with people—I could feel it.

"My book is all about questions. Questions are incredibly powerful. They are the secret to happiness, to success, to life." I paused as I reached one side of the stage and turned to walk back toward the center. "But there is *one* question that is the most powerful question you can ask. It is the *most important* question you can ask. It is the *one* question that can help you no matter where you are on your journey or what you're looking for. It's the one question that *everyone* wants to know the answers to."

I stopped center stage, and faced the audience full on. "Do you want to know what that question is?"

This time there was a resounding "Yesss!" from around the arena.

"That question," I said, forcing myself to slow down to make sure they all heard it, "is this."

I kept my voice calm but strong. I said it slowly, deliberately, and with as much passion as I could put into my now even-keeled voice. "How can I live a better life?"

I paused. No one spoke. I could sense the disappointment. "*But*," I said quickly. "That question, as important as it is . . . is not nearly as important as the answers." I started walking back and forth again, my voice speeding up.

"And now"—I looked at my watch—"for the next twelve minutes"—I paused again and looked around the auditorium, from one side all the way to the other—"I'm going to give you those answers."

The more I talked, the more passionate I became. I couldn't help myself. It was as though all the years of wanting to help other people had been built up inside of me, and suddenly the dam had broken. It all came out. I couldn't remember exactly what I said, or how I said it, but I know I was excited. I talked fast; my hands were waving all over the place. I even jumped straight up in the air at one point.

When my remaining twelve minutes were up, I finished my last thought. Then, when the audience was as quiet as an audience can be in an arena that size, I said, "That's all the time I have. Thank you very much for listening."

For a brief second, I thought they hadn't heard me. It seemed to me like an eternally long, awkward silence, though Holly assured me later that it had only felt that way to me. Then, suddenly, what sounded like a few small bursts of applause quickly became a thunderous stage-rattling crescendo. I stood there in awe as the house lights came on and everyone got to their feet to give me a standing ovation.

The emcee came out and put his arm around me like we were long-lost friends.

"Was that amazing or what?" he goaded the audience, sending them into an even louder round of applause. At one point, with his arm still draped around my shoulder as if sharing in the accolades, he tried to get them to quiet down so he could tell them what to expect next in the program. It only caused the audience to renew their fervor with whistles and more applause.

I stood there, slightly embarrassed, as the emcee dropped his arm from my shoulder, took a few steps, and turned to face me, joining in with the audience and clapping. I waved awkwardly and began making my way toward the side of the stage.

When I stepped out of the spotlight and passed the floor director who, incredibly, was also clapping, I saw Holly. She was crying and smiling at the same time. She ran up the steps and threw her arms around me. "*That*," she said, "was amazing!"

I was still floating and riding the wave of energy from the audience and didn't know what to say. Eventually, I said, "I need to go to the bathroom."

Holly broke off her hug and laughed.

We exited the backstage area. She helped me find a men's room, telling me she was going to the event's bookstore room to make sure the four boxes of books she had sent had at least arrived. She was going to make sure they put a few on display, even if she had to open the boxes and do it herself.

I went into the men's room and approached the sink, turning on some cold water and splashing my face. The lights on the stage had been hot, and I realized I'd been sweating quite a bit. I looked up into the mirror and took in my reflection.

Well, I thought as I looked at the face I'd been gazing at for almost fifty years, *I did it.* No matter what happened from here on out, no one could say I hadn't tried. I was also exhausted.

I dried my face and went back into the hallway, ready to search for Holly and the bookstore room. Instead, I found her running toward me from the end of the long hallway, shouting, "Oliver! Oliver! Come quick. You have to see this."

"What?" I said as she came sliding to a halt before me.

"Come on," she said, grabbing my arm and pulling me behind her as she set off running in the direction she had just come from. "You won't believe it."

She burst through the doors at the end of the hallway. Again, I asked her what was going on, but she ignored my pleas. We were now back in the larger hallway of the hotel, and she led me, half running, down the red-carpeted expanse, around two corners, and into a much wider atrium near the arena's front entrances.

People were emerging from multiple doors to my left as they exited the arena and descended stairs into the large open space below. In front of me, a line of people seemed to snake back and forth twice before disappearing around a corner off to the right. Holly pushed forward into the throng, pulling me with her, and we began half running, half weaving down the hallway, parallel to the queue. As we rounded the corner, the line continued and doubled back on itself again before entering a set of double doors on our right. Holly rushed up to the open doors and pulled me behind her. She squeezed by some people standing in line, saying, "Sorry, excuse us. Sorry, pardon us."

I was sure we were going to get yelled at, but as we passed, I felt a few pats on my shoulder and heard one or two people saying, "Hey, it's him."

Once inside the room, I could see it was a smaller hotel ballroom that had been converted into the event's bookstore. Several tables were off to the right, forming two rows of aisles and piled with various books for sale.

At the back was another long table with three people behind it; they appeared to be acting as cashiers. The line of people we had passed was now being pushed to the left side of the room as hotel staff set up red-roped stanchions to cordon them off. In front of where the line ended, another hotel staff member was wrapping draping around the front of another folding table that had just been set up. As I looked closely, I saw someone else opening boxes on top of the table.

Pulling Holly's hand to bring her to a stop, I asked, "What's going on?"

She turned, smiled a smile bigger than I'd ever seen her smile before, and gestured to the line snaking out the door. "They all want to buy your book."

I'm sure I must have looked like a complete fool, because I just stood there with my mouth open, unable to speak. I looked at the line and then back at the table at the front. I saw the staff member pulling out copies of my book and placing them on the table. Another staff member joined her and began setting up a laptop and what looked like a small credit card machine at the head of the table.

I looked back at Holly, who was still grinning like a child at Christmas. She followed my gaze, and her smile turned into a worried frown. "There's only one problem," she said.

"What?" I croaked out of my suddenly dry throat. She looked up and gazed into my face with worry, but also with restrained excitement. "We don't have enough books."

I looked at the table. She was right. She said she had sent four boxes, which meant a hundred copies of my book—a number that yesterday I would have said was optimistically ambitious. Looking back at the line and remembering what we had seen in the atrium as we raced by, I knew there were at least five times that many people in line already and more had been joining the queue as we passed.

One of the event staff came over and asked Holly if there were any more books. When Holly told her no, she looked at the line and said what we were all thinking: "Oh dear!" Then she turned to me and asked if I would sign those that were bought from the table they had just set up. They could place a chair at the other end, and as people bought them, they could get in another line to have me sign them.

I couldn't believe what she was saying. I couldn't believe people were queued by the hundreds to buy my book, much less that they would want me to sign them. I simply nodded.

Holly then asked what would happen when they ran out of books.

There was an uncomfortable pause before the event staffer said they'd just have to turn everyone away once that happened.

My mind was racing. Holly looked at me with a shocked expression. We were both thinking the same thing. We couldn't turn all these people away, but we had no more books. I had to ask myself different questions.

How can we give these people what they want when we have no more books?

The staffer went to set up the signing station.

I turned to Holly. "Find some paper. Index cards would be ideal, but if not, get someone to cut some paper down to about that size."

"Why?" she asked.

"Do you think Arthur would ship books at the discounted price they're selling for here?" I asked.

"I don't know. I guess so. Why?" she asked, but then she seemed to get the idea. "We'll just take orders and ship them later," she said, getting excited. "So, the paper is for their addresses."

"Yes," I said, "and no."

She looked up at me, clearly confused. "Then what is the paper for?"

"Look." I moved toward the table where people were already buying the book and then getting in the second line for signatures . . . unreal. "We can't let these people stand in line to buy the book and then have to wait to get it. They'll just as likely get out of line once the first hundred are gone." I had almost reached the table. "What if I stay to meet them, and if they give me the name of the person they want the book signed to, I'll sign them before we ship them?"

"What," she said, looking back at the line, "all of them?"

"Sure, why not?"

She pulled me aside so as not to be heard by the people nearby. "Oliver, that line is probably over six hundred people strong by now, and it could grow even longer."

I smiled at her. "I know, crazy, isn't it?"

She smiled back. "Yes, it is, but you could be here for hours just meeting them, and then you'll have to sign all those books before they get shipped. You'll have to come to the office to do that. It could take hours or days, and . . ."

I could see she was getting caught up in the details of it all. I knew it would be a lot of work, but that didn't matter.

"Holly," I said, interrupting her stream of thought, "I know. I know it will be a lot to do, but it's the right thing to do." I paused and then said, "If they're willing to wait in that line, it's the least I can do."

She shook her head and then looked up at me with a smile. "You are amazing, you know that?"

"Go find some paper," I replied, and turned toward the signing table as she set off on her errand.

Chapter 14
Shockwaves

The next few days were a blur. Holly had been right—the line had grown to over a thousand people. I signed the first hundred books. Afterward, I stayed to greet everyone who "preordered" a signed copy using the index cards Holly had snared from the event bookstore staff. I met people of all ages, shook hands, heard their stories, and even took some photos with them. It was wonderful, amazing, and exhausting.

Holly had already talked to her uncle, who began gathering copies from the rest of the first print run. He was pretty sure they would have enough to cover what ended up being 1,076 additional orders for signed copies. She also called the airline and changed our flight to the latest possible one back to Denver that night. Even so, we left the convention after I said hello to the last couple in line, Mr. and Mrs. Poole from Kokomo, Indiana, and got to our gate just as the last section was boarding. Holly collapsed in her seat and fell asleep almost instantly. Normally, I can sleep on planes, but although I was exhausted, my mind was too wound up to let me rest.

I opened my front door just past midnight to a happy but barking Marlow and a nice welcome-home note from our dog sitter. I sent a text to Mary telling her it was too late to call now (it was well past two in the morning her time) but that I would call her the next day to catch up. Holly had flown back to Denver with me because she said we needed to plan for signing all the books, and it would be easier for her to do it tomorrow from there. I had offered to put her up in our spare room, but she said she would check in to the newly opened hotel at the airport.

The next morning, after only a few hours of sleep, Mary called me and I told her all about the event. Because of the time difference on the East Coast, she had called at four o'clock in the morning—six o'clock her time. She was astounded when I told her what happened, and even more upset that she missed it all. I told her about needing to go to Dallas to sign the copies. She said she would get a hold of the dog sitter to watch Marlow for another day or two. So, that afternoon, I boarded another flight and headed to Arthur's house outside of Dallas, as he had insisted that I stay with him and Holly while I was there.

We had a celebratory dinner and raised a glass of wine in honor of the event. The next morning, at the offices of PenBridge Publishing, I sat down at a comfortable desk with just under eleven hundred index cards and books and began signing. Holly, Arthur, and their assistant, Jeanne, wrapped, boxed, and addressed the books to be mailed. It was a long day, with a working lunch and a short break to go out to a local Tex-Mex restaurant that Arthur liked, but by midday the following day, we had all the books signed and sealed, with the last batch ready to go out in the mail. I fell asleep as soon as we got back to Arthur's home and didn't wake up until nearly nine o'clock the following morning.

It was Sunday afternoon of the next weekend when Holly called. Mary and I were sitting on our front porch having a drink—coffee for her, tea for me. Marlow was running around the front yard, chasing birds, and occasionally lying down to enjoy the fresh morning air. Mary was on her iPad looking at shoes when my cell phone rang.

"Hello, Holly," I said, looking at the caller ID.

"Have you seen it?" she asked, her voice high-pitched with excitement.

"Seen what?" I asked cautiously.

"The *New York Times*," she said, then, "Look in the book review section, next to the last page."

I had already read our copy of the *Times*, and while I sometimes looked at the book review section, I hadn't that morning, focusing only on a few sections of the paper that I normally read, like the magazine and opinion sections. "Why?"

"Just look," she answered cryptically. "Don't you get the *Times*?"

"Yeah, sure," I said as I picked up the paper that was on the little porch table between our chairs. Mary looked over at me as I grabbed the book review section and turned to the next to last page.

It appeared that a reporter for the *Times* had attended the event in San Diego to write a piece about home-based businesses. Instead, he had written a different piece altogether. The title read "WRITER STEALS SHOW WITH 15 POWER-PACKED MINUTES." The reporter, a fellow named Josh Lindstrom—*why did that name sound familiar to me?*—began by describing his experience at the event, but then said how he had stood in line to buy my book and had been one of the over one thousand who had preordered a signed copy.

That's why his name sounded familiar: I had signed one of the books to him in Dallas.

Mr. Lindstrom went on to say how he had been surprised to receive his signed copy four days after the event, asking, "Who signs books days after events are over these days, never mind turning them around that quickly?" He also said that he couldn't put the book down once he opened it.

He mentioned a few points in the book that he thought could be improved, but overall, he gave it a rave review.

Mary and I talked with Holly on speakerphone for half an hour, amazed at this surprise review. "This is powerful, Oliver," Holly said. "You can't pay for this kind of advertising."

I laughed. "Well," I said, "hopefully this will help a few more people by exposing them to the ideas."

"Who knows," Mary said, "maybe it will sell another hundred copies."

We all laughed. We had no idea.

It was Arthur who called me the following Friday. He was so excited he could hardly get the words out. "They're all calling or writing or emailing—they want more."

"Who?" I asked cautiously. "Who wants more? What are you talking about?" I didn't dare entertain what I thought he was saying.

"Stores!" he shouted in excitement. "Amazon, Barnes and Noble, distributors—they all want more books." And then he said the words that left me speechless: "They're all sold out."

He said that he was already printing a second run and, with the way the orders were coming in, would likely need a third by the end of the month.

Later that afternoon, Holly called to say they were getting requests from radio shows and magazines wanting to interview me. Over the next few weeks, my inbox flooded with emails from readers. They thanked me for the book, asked their own questions of me, and told me about ideas they had for new questions to ask. I began spending a great deal of time answering their messages and working on the website, trying to create a forum where readers could talk among themselves and share ideas.

By the following month, I had been interviewed on four internet radio programs and was scheduled for two live radio programs in Colorado. Holly called again to say that one of the Denver television stations wanted me to appear on their afternoon program, and a Dallas station wanted me to do an interview as well. She and Arthur were also getting requests to have me speak for associations and at conventions.

Book sales were continuing to grow, and Arthur had just finished his third printing run. My book was climbing the Amazon bestseller list, and Holly said, "Rumor has it you might be on the *New York Times* list by the end of next month."

Arthur and Holly arranged a book and speaking tour with Mary, and I soon traveled the country for book signings in every manner of bookstore imaginable—from large multistory stores in New York to small mom-and-pop shops in New Hampshire and San Francisco.

It was exhausting and tedious, but it was exhilarating and amazing every time. I met incredible people whose lives, they said, had been changed by my book. An amateur video of my fifteen-minute talk at the San Diego arena, taken by someone in the audience on their smartphone, made its way to YouTube and became a viral sensation.

Doug and Alison called one day from Africa to say they had just watched it and had even heard on their local news about my book's amazing success. After Alison and Mary finished catching up, I got a few minutes with Doug on the phone.

"Well," he said, "look at you now."

"Yeah," I said, with an embarrassed laugh, "it's all a little crazy, buddy."

"You deserve it," he said. "You sound a lot happier than the last time I saw you."

I thought back to that ride to the airport when he and Alison left for Africa. It seemed a lifetime ago.

"Hey," he said, interrupting my thoughts, "have you seen Violet lately?"

"No," I said, "I've been so busy. I should send her an email."

"Well," he said, "when you see her, tell her hello for me, will you?"

"I will," I said, "seriously, if it hadn't been for you introducing me to her, none of this would have ever happened."

We said goodbye, promised to find some way to get together in the future, and hung up the phone.

It seemed we couldn't go a week without some amazing news from Arthur or Holly. Arthur called one morning to say he was getting requests from overseas to have the book translated. He assured me he and Holly were working on the international rights and securing translators, and I hung up feeling ever more grateful that this small publisher had believed in me.

Holly, it seemed, was moving up from Austin to live in the Dallas–Fort Worth area so she could be closer to the business, and they were hiring two more people. Word had gotten out, and authors, both new and established, were clamoring to be published by PenBridge.

Our lives were changing, and I could no longer keep up with all the daily emails. Mary had found an intern, a young woman from a local college, who was helping to sort through the flood in my inbox so I could respond appropriately.

Our first few royalty checks were enough to get us through the rest of the year, and Arthur assured me that many more were coming my way. "I hope you're already working on your next book," he said one afternoon on our now-weekly calls. "I'm already getting questions about when they can expect it."

Next book? *Good grief,* I thought. It had taken almost everything out of me to write this book. I didn't think I had anything left to say.

And just like that, the beginning of an idea rumbled in my mind. I knew exactly what I would write next.

Chapter 15
The Institute

I drove around the winding corners with a curiosity I hadn't felt in some time. The sun was shining on the tall evergreens that cascaded down the mountainsides all around me. I drove easily, no longer feeling the urgency I once had, trying to get from place to place, always in a hurry.

It was a pleasant drive. As I came around the next bend, I saw a raging stream to my right, full of snowmelt from the winter's runoff, and the steep mountainside I had been driving beside suddenly gave way to a beautiful valley. The stream broke off beside my road and cut a path through a lush, grassy area. A dark wooden split-rail fence was visible here and there, though it seemed less for boundary and more for aesthetics, as though someone had put it there to create the image of a painting or the perfect setting for a postcard photograph.

I followed the winding road to the other side of this picturesque valley, and it was only then, as the road climbed again, that I noticed the building. It was massive; even from this distance I could see that. It hung on the edge of a rocky precipice, overlooking the valley like some sort of outpost.

I continued up the road and took the exit marked by a simple sign, which hung between two stone posts and was supported by black wrought-iron chains on a wooden beam. It read "The Living Prism Institute." My mind rewound to the brief—and somewhat mysterious—call I had made a few weeks before. I had not been to the Denver Grill in some time, my life having become one series of trips, speaking engagements, and new adventures, speckled here and there with stints of writing.

I had called Gerald one afternoon and asked him if he had a phone number for Violet, as she had not answered my last few emails. He apologized and said he had no number or address for her. He remembered she had once mentioned her work, something about a "Life Colors Institute" or some such thing. He apologized profusely for not being more helpful and assured me that if he saw or heard from Violet, he would pass on the message that I was trying to reach her.

I scoured the internet for a "Life Color Institute," to no avail. I tried various combinations and searches but could find nothing. Just as I was about to give in, one of my searches produced a brief article about a Life Prism Institute in the Rocky Mountains of Colorado. The article from the local town newspaper discussed how the Institute had built a beautiful facility, and anyone wishing to tour the new building could do so by calling the number provided.

I tried more searches for "The Life Prism Institute" and could find neither a website nor any reference to the company. Out of sheer curiosity, I called the number from the article, now five years old, not really expecting anything. After responding to an initial query as to who I was, I asked if someone by the name of Violet worked there. I was astonished when the woman who answered the telephone put me on hold and a gentleman with a heavy British accent came on the line.

"Hello, Mr. Goodwin?" he inquired.

"Yes," I replied.

"Ah," he said. "My name is Jeffery Holbourn, I'm the director of the Institute. I understand you were inquiring about Violet?"

"Yes," I said awkwardly, "I'm just trying to reach her, and to be honest, I have no idea how to." I told him about my meetings with her at the Denver Grill and how Gerald had led me to search the internet and ultimately call the number.

"Yes," he said slowly. "Yes, I see." He went on, "Well, she does indeed work here at the Institute." He paused. "But she's been out of the country for some months, which is likely why you haven't heard from her."

"Oh," I said sadly, "Do you know when she will be back?"

"Not for quite some time, I'm afraid."

I didn't know what to say and was about to thank him and ring off when he said, "Actually, I was wondering if you'd like to come by the Institute?" Before I could answer, he added, "To be honest, it would be an honor to meet you. I've read your work, and I am a big fan."

I thanked him, and we arranged for me to come and see him the following week. He gave me explicit directions, and so it was that I parked in the lot among a smattering of other cars and walked into what could only be described as the nicest ski-lodge-like building I have ever seen.

Inside the lobby, I announced who I was and said I had an appointment with Mr. Holbourn. I looked around as I waited in the comfortable leather armchairs suited for the purpose. I found myself in a large A-framed hall, with real log walls and large wooden beams on the ceiling. A warm, crackling fireplace was set against the far end, with a gray stone chimney that extended to the roof and beyond.

A tall man I guessed to be in his late fifties came forward and put out his hand. "Mr. Goodwin, I'm Jeffery Holbourn. It's a pleasure to meet you."

I shook his hand. His grip was firm. Slightly taller than my six-foot frame, he was lanky, with a full head of white hair and clear blue eyes. He motioned for me to follow him, and he led me down a hallway with large picture windows that overlooked the valley below. The view was breathtaking. I followed him up a set of stairs bordered by large plate-glass windows. I was more than a little unnerved, as I wasn't the fondest of heights, and the windows afforded me a view of just how close to the edge of the cliff the building was perched on.

I avoided visibly shaking, and we arrived at the second-floor corner office that Mr. Holbourn's title commanded. A curved wall of glass offered a jaw-dropping view of the landscape below.

I remarked on the beauty of both the building and his office view.

He smiled. "Yes, it's spectacular, isn't it?" he said. Then he added, "Sometimes I have to turn my desk away from the windows just to get something done."

We laughed good-naturedly, and he offered me a seat in one of two armchairs facing his desk and the window. He took the other chair and turned it toward me.

"I expect you're more than a little curious about us," he began, waving his arm to indicate the Institute and the building we were in.

I nodded. "Yes, just a little," I said. "To be honest, I'm also curious about what Violet does here."

He nodded as if to himself. "Did she tell you anything about herself or of her position at the Institute?"

Embarrassed, I said, "No. I'm afraid I know very little about her at all."

He nodded again, as if expecting this answer. Then he placed his fingertips together and rested his chin on them, as if considering what to say next. I waited patiently for him to begin.

After a few moments, he looked at me and smiled. "Violet's parents died when she was quite young," he said. "I was her father's best friend, and with no other relatives, her guardianship fell to me.

I leaned back and crossed my legs as he continued his story. "She was only just out of diapers when it happened, and it wasn't long after that I noticed . . . irregularities . . . in her behavior." He smiled again, as though recalling a distant memory. "I won't bore you with the details, but the doctors began testing her and found that she fell on the autism spectrum, but her differences went beyond that. The long and short of it is that she is quite brilliant."

I, of course, knew how intelligent she was. The comment about the autism spectrum was surprising, yet it explained so much.

Jeffery continued, "She is brilliant in ways we simply cannot understand." He noticed my frown and added, "It's quite difficult to explain, I'm afraid, but suffice it to say her mind is off the charts . . . *multiple* charts." He went on. "In a prior life I worked in the pharmaceutical industry, and I reached out to some friends who reached out to other friends, and, well, we found some doctors in Zurich who have been helping her through some new trial medications to both control and harness her incredible mind."

I wasn't sure I entirely understood what he was telling me, but I nodded, as hearing this seemed to put pieces of a jigsaw puzzle together in my head.

"It's where she is now," he said. "In Zurich. You see, this . . ."—he waved his hand around again—"is all hers."

This time I cocked my head the way Marlow did at home. I'm sure with an even more quizzical look than I had before. "What do you mean, all hers?"

Again, Jeffery rested his chin on his fingertips and looked over at me. "Her mind sees things, understands things, in unique ways." His eyes narrowed as he went on. "She can see patterns in the financial markets, see potential in entrepreneurial ventures, and I daresay, even with people." He nodded at me.

"I'm not sure I understand," I said slowly.

"When we first learned of her . . . condition . . . we weren't sure what it meant. It helped us explain some of her behaviors, and she had a little more of an idea about why her mind worked the way it did, but . . ." He giggled. "Now what?"

He continued. "One summer, she would have been about twelve, she began reading financial papers, studying stock markets, doing analysis. Something about the numbers 'spoke' to her." He made air quotes when he said the word "spoke." "I didn't think much of it at the time, but over the course of a few months, she began talking about different companies, bonds, stocks, et cetera, and soon I began seeing those same names pop up in the news."

He looked at me with his eyebrows raised. "It didn't take me long to figure out she was able to pick winners and losers the same way you and I pick good bananas from bad ones."

I smiled back at him, waiting for him to continue his tale. He told me that by the time Violet was sixteen, they had invested in several companies and were making a sizable fortune from her financial prowess. At first, he had used the money to pay off medical bills and the house they were living in. He looked at me seriously when he said that at one point, he began to worry about how much money they were actually making and whether they might get in trouble with the authorities.

"Violet was never one to sit still," Jeffery said, "and just as soon as her interest in the markets had started, it stopped." He paused and looked down at his clasped hands before looking back up at me. "She took more of an interest in people. She couldn't get enough of them. She came to me one day and said she wanted to start this Institute to help people, to invest in ideas and help the world." Again, he laughed fondly, like he was back in that time, in a memory that made him smile.

"We worked together on the plans, going over the blueprints and designing all the details." His smile faded a little now. "I wish she were here to see it more." His voice was soft now, wistful.

"I don't understand," I said.

"I see little of her anymore, I'm afraid," he said bluntly. "Ever since she turned eighteen, she's become . . ." He paused, looking for the right word. "A vagabond, I suppose."

He looked at me and saw the perplexity in my expression. "She feels most at home wandering," he said. "She has access to her accounts, so I know she'll never want for anything, but this"—again he waved an arm suggesting our surroundings—"is not somewhere she can stay for long."

Jeffery told me that the biggest challenge she still faced was not just her lack of social skills, which, of course, I knew firsthand, but her complete energy breakdowns, which apparently happened about once a month. She could function well for up to three weeks, but at some point the following week, she would collapse on the spot. One minute she would appear normal, and the next her entire body would shut down as though it had used up every ounce of energy over the previous three weeks.

Jeffery's demeanor changed, and a genuine look of care and concern crossed his face as he told me he often didn't know where she was. Her "lifestyle" was that of a nomad, and she often wandered from place to place for days or weeks without him knowing where she was. He told me once he had been called by a friend who had seen her living in a homeless shelter, but when he had arrived to collect her, she had already left. Clearly, he was worried about her condition and what might happen if no one was there to take care of her.

"Somehow, some way," he said, "she always seems to come back."

Sometimes a stranger would drive her to the Institute, and occasionally he would receive a call, but more often than not, she would simply walk in one day as if her absence was nothing out of the ordinary.

"Such is life with Violet," he said, smiling. "And that's the thing." His eyes now beamed with pride. "She makes all of us feel better, live better, and do better." I could see he believed deeply in what he was saying. "She brings an energy to life that I wish I could bottle. Is she quirky? Yes. Is she different? Absolutely." And then, with a smile that lit up his face, he added, "Quite frankly, I wish more people were as different as Violet."

I knew what he meant. It was hard to describe, but once you got past her lack of social graces and her no-nonsense conversational manner, you always left feeling more alive than you had been before you saw her.

Jeffery interrupted my thoughts with, "She's incredibly proud of you, you know."

I wasn't sure what to say to that, though I suddenly felt very pleased to know that she was proud of me.

"I've heard her talk about only a few of her world friends," he said, "and I use the term 'world friends' because that's what she calls you. Anyway, although she's mentioned one or two here and there when I see or speak to her, she's never talked about anyone as much as you."

He leaned forward a little. "She sent me a copy of your book the day it came out and told me I needed to make it 'required reading'"—he held up his air quotes as he said it—"for the staff at the Institute," and then he added with a smile, "which it is."

We talked a little longer, mostly about Violet. He asked me what she was like when she was with me, how often I had seen her, et cetera. Finally, our conversation slowed down and I stood to take my leave.

I thanked him for his time, and for telling me his and Violet's story. As I turned to go, he reached around his desk and brought out a large paper bag with handles, the kind you get at a department store, though this one bore no label. Passing the handles to me, he said, "This arrived for you yesterday. I mentioned to Violet in an email earlier this week that you would be coming by, and she apparently had this shipped the next day."

I opened the bag and saw a box inside, wrapped in white paper and tied with a dark red ribbon. "Thank you," I said.

We exchanged contact information, and he promised to get in touch with me if he heard Violet was back in the States.

I drove down the mountain, taking in all the beautiful scenery and reflecting on how much my life had changed since that day when I first met Violet. I thought about all the stress I had left behind in creating this new life for Mary and me. Not that we didn't have any stress; it was just a different kind now. Manageable, normal stress, not the kind that can kill you.

I thought about how Violet had helped me figure out what to write and how to write it, and then, through Arthur and Holly, how to get it published. Now I was speaking to audiences, teaching people how to live better lives. It all seemed so surreal.

I walked into the house and said hello to Mary. She wanted to know how the visit had gone and all the details, but just as I began telling her, the phone rang. She picked it up and said, "Oh, hello, Holly."

Her face became serious, and then a huge grin broke out and she practically shouted, "What?"

Then, telling Holly to hold on, she jumped up and down as she told me that an international publisher wanted to translate the book into three languages and that they saw potential in several other markets. As if that wasn't big enough news, her voice rose even higher as she added, "And that's not all." Pausing for a moment, she looked at me with her big bright eyes and said, "The BBC wants to do a story on you. They want you to come to London! Holly and Arthur are working on a speaking tour while we're there!"

She turned back to the phone, saying to Holly, "Yes, yes, he's thrilled . . ."

I thought the more appropriate response would have been "He's astonished," but I just shook my head in disbelief as I climbed the stairs to what was now my office as Mary and Holly shrieked and laughed on the phone like two little schoolgirls. Nothing surprised me anymore. Well, almost nothing.

I sat down in my comfortable chair, exhausted. It had been a long day. A good day, for sure, but emotionally draining. I had learned so much about Violet, and now it looked like a new adventure was about to begin overseas.

I rubbed Marlow behind the ears as he sat panting beside me. I reached down and pulled the box out of the bag Jeffery had given me. Once again, I marveled at how my life had changed. I had been so afraid to follow my dream, and here I was living it. It seemed there was no limit to the wonderful things that could happen once I had the courage to jump off the edge of that cliff.

I knew I owed a lot to Holly and Arthur, and to Violet, and, of course, to Mary. I would never have been able to do any of this if she hadn't been around to keep me going when I'd wanted to give up.

I pulled at the ribbon and slid it off the box.

I thought back to that first spark of an idea I'd had so long ago. To the moment I had actually started to write and how frightened I'd been that no one would want to read what I was writing.

I pulled the lid off the box, and as I peeled back the delicate dark red tissue paper inside, I thought about all the ripple effects my actions had created. I thought about how the faith that Mary, Violet, Arthur, and Holly had put in me was truly all I had needed. How they had known just how and when to push me, and at the same time when to encourage me, was still a mystery. I wondered how many of Violet's other "world friends" she had helped and what she was doing at that moment. I wondered if her treatments were working. I wondered if she knew just how much she had transformed my life.

I peered at what was wrapped in the tissue paper, and my world came to a crashing halt.

I couldn't think. I couldn't hear a sound. I could barely breathe.

My mind was exploding.

I sat motionless, staring at the contents of the box. *This isn't possible.*

There was no note.

Inside the box, resting on the soft tissue paper, was a pair of bright red EVERLAST boxing gloves.

The Five Answers

Thank you, thank you very much.

I wrote a book about questions. About how questions can empower every area of your life. I was supposed to talk to you this afternoon, and I had hoped to tell you everything that was in the book. Give you all the tools, all the secrets, everything, so that you would leave here and be able to implement them immediately! But then the organizers of this incredible event came to me and said they needed to rearrange the lineup, and they asked me if there was any way I could help them. They wondered if I could switch my time slot, and instead of what I had originally planned, they wanted me to give you something better. Something even more powerful and more impactful than my original presentation, and they wanted me to do it in *fifteen minutes*!

I said, "Absolutely, I have *just the thing*!" So, are you *ready?*

OK, get out your notebooks because *here we go*!

My book is all about questions. Questions are incredibly powerful. They're the secret to happiness, to success, to life, but there is *one* question that is the most powerful question you can ask. It is the *most important* question you can ask.

It is the *one* question that can help you no matter where you are in your journey or what you're looking for. It's the one question that *everyone* wants to know the answer to. Do you want to know what that question is?

That question is this: How can I live a better life? But, that question, as important as it is. . . is not nearly as important as the answers, and now, for the next twelve minutes, I'm going to give you those answers.

NUMBER ONE

The first answer is something I call **The Responsibility of Gratitude!**

There is a Hawaiian word *kuleana*, which is difficult to translate into English, but I once heard someone from Hawaii define it as "with any right or privilege comes a sense of obligation or responsibility." Each of us has a right to a better life, to live the life we want and dream of. We are privileged to live in a world and time that allows us to determine our life the way we want it to be. With that privilege, however, comes responsibility—the responsibility of gratitude. The two are linked, and indeed, one drives the other and vice versa.

You must be grateful for—and appreciate—what you have in your life right now before you can earn the privilege of having more. Put another way, you cannot take the next step in your journey of life until you step fully and completely into the step you are taking right now.

Most people see gratitude only in terms of what they have. They wake up and think, "I am grateful for all that I have." This is good, but it is not all that gratitude encompasses. You must be grateful for what you *are*, not only what you have. Don't complain about the past, it's what made you who you are today. Don't worry about the future. You have the capacity to create the future you want. The key is that you must recognize and appreciate your present and be grateful for all that it is.

Be grateful for the relationships you have—personally, professionally, and informally. Don't dwell on relationships that have soured or on people who have wronged you in some way. Be grateful for all your experiences with every relationship you have had and currently have. Only then can you fully expect and receive new relationships or make changes to current ones.

Be grateful for the health you have today, right now. Regardless of what ails you or any health concerns you may have, be grateful that you are *alive* today! Embrace that gratitude in this moment so you can free yourself up to work on positive health changes in the future.

Be grateful for the body you have, not the body you wish you had. Your actions today will determine the body you have tomorrow—and the day after that—and the one after that. You cannot expect to improve your body if you first do not appreciate the one you have today.

You have the right, the expectation, and the privilege of having a Better Life. You also have the responsibility of being grateful for what you have received every moment of your life up to this point. Be grateful for everything, and watch everything change—for the better.

Wake up each day with gratitude. Be honestly, truly, and completely grateful for your life. Once you can master being grateful for the life you have, you immediately begin to create the life you want to have—a Better Life!

NUMBER TWO

The second answer is to **Leave Your Fingerprints!**

Each one of you has a unique set of fingerprints. That means there is no one exactly like you. You are one of a kind. There is no one who thinks like you, who experiences life the way you do, and who sees things like you. That also means that no one has the same passions as you, and no one has the same dreams you do.

Only you can leave your unique set of fingerprints.

Only *you* can discover your *passions*. And only you can achieve your *dreams*.

Ellen Goodman once said, "Normal is getting dressed in clothes that you buy for work, driving through traffic in a car that you are still paying for, in order to get to a job that you need so you can pay for the clothes, car and the house that you leave empty all day in order to afford to live in it."

You are given your passions for a reason. Your dreams are your calling. It's up to you to decide whether to follow them. Most people live the normal life Ms. Goodman spoke of. Most people never discover their true passions or follow their dreams. The reasons are many, but the consequences are the same: By failing to discover your passions and achieve your dreams, you deprive not only yourself, but the world, of all that you are capable of.

There are 168 hours in a week, of which you will sleep approximately 56 hours, leaving you with 112 waking hours every week. How will you spend those hours? Will you spend them doing something that "pays the bills" or something that makes your *soul dance*?

Will you create a life built on passion and purpose? Will you dare to dream as you once did when you were a child and the world was full of possibilities?

Seth Godin is famous for saying that "Instead of wondering when your next vacation is, maybe you should set up a life you don't need to escape from."

Many people believe that chasing your dreams is futile Pollyannaish nonsense. The fact is that it's not a question of whether you will chase your dreams.

You have two choices. You can build your dream or build someone else's. It's that simple.

Leave your own fingerprints and stop helping someone else leave theirs. Your fingerprints, your passions and dreams, are your blueprint to living a Better Life!

NUMBER THREE

The third answer is to **Live the HIGH life!**

OK, OK, you can stop giggling now. I know I'm from Colorado, but I'm not talking about that kind of high.

The short answer to the high life I'm talking about is to always do the right thing.

The first "H" in my version of "high life" stands for Honor. It's doing what you say you're going to do. It means keeping your word.

The "I" stands for Integrity, which by my definition means standing by your word even if no one will know that you did. That's one of the hardest parts of this "high life" and probably the most important one.

The "G" in "HIGH" stands for having your life Guided by your heart and soul. When you stop and really think about it, you know if something is right or wrong. You can *feel* it. That's your soul talking to you. When you aren't sure what to do, all you have to do is find a space to be quiet, to let your mind relax, and let your heart lead you. Between the two—your heart and your soul—you'll always know the right way to proceed, and they'll never steer you wrong.

The last "H" in this principle of the "high life" stands for Honesty. Unfortunately, too many people have forgotten what real honesty means these days. Lies, although they can sometimes bring about temporary success, don't have a long shelf life, and sooner or later the truth comes out—usually at a much higher price than being honest would have cost from the beginning.

You might think this "high life" is simply another version of "treat others the way you want to be treated," and while it certainly includes the Golden Rule, it's much more than that.

It means that when you have to choose between helping the company make a little more profit or helping the customer with what's in their best interest, choose the latter because it's the right thing to do.

It means that when someone you care about needs you and you've got more "important" things to do, stop and let your heart and soul help you make the best decision.

Be true to yourself, follow the path your heart leads you down, and don't let others' opinions hold you back. What other people think of you is, after all, none of your business. You can either choose to give negative thoughts a room to live in, or you can shut the door on them and allow space for positive thoughts to enter.

With every person you encounter, focus on what the best outcome would be for both of you. Be honest in all that you do, and live and work with integrity and honor always. Trust your heart, listen to your soul, and soon you will find yourself living a Better Life!

NUMBER FOUR

The fourth answer is to **Be a GOMER!**

Now, before you start thinking that I've lost my marbles, understand that I was a big fan of *The Andy Griffith Show*, for those of you old enough to remember the reference.

In this case, however, GOMER stands for Give Others More than you Expect to Receive. GOMER.

You may have heard of this before, and people often say that you must give more than you receive. But have you ever heard of the adage that when you help someone or give more to others that it will come back to you tenfold?

Well, then, it would be pretty hard to give more than you receive if every time you gave you got back ten times what you had given, right? That's why it's all about giving more than you *expect* to receive.

Now, most people think this means doing more than you get paid to do at work, and certainly that's one way to apply this principle. It is a long-standing rule of success that doing more than you are financially compensated for will bring you more success. However, this applies to much more than simply your work. It means giving more than you expect to receive in everything you do: in your relationships, in your interactions with other people, and in your day-to-day activities.

You see, we don't always receive what we think we will—or put another way, what we *expect* to receive. Sometimes it's more, sometimes it's less. Sometimes we receive in ways that we never thought possible.

Maybe you are in retail and your products are sold for more than it costs to make them but less than they are worth. Thereby, the items have more value than the money you receive for them. When someone buys one of your products, you expect to receive the price you charge for it and that's all. The customer gets something for less than its actual value, and you make a profit. However, the unforeseen effect of doing business this way is that the customer is so pleased by their purchase that they begin telling everyone they know about it. Unbeknownst to you, more and more business is generated by that sale than would have happened without it. You are receiving more than you expected, whether you know it or not.

Imagine loving your partner more than you expect them to love you. Now imagine them doing the same back to you—what would *that* relationship be like? What if you gave more to your friends than you expected them to give back, in terms of your friendship, your time, your love? What if you listened more than you talked? Remember that listening is not the act of silence in anticipation of your turn to speak, but the absence of thought other than what the other person is saying.

What if you cared about other people more than you expected them to care about you? What if you took a genuine interest in the people who serve you at coffee shops, restaurants, and department stores, without expecting them to give anything in return? Wouldn't your interactions become more meaningful, more interesting, and more enjoyable?

What would your life be like if you made it your mission every day to help other people more than you expected them to help you—to focus more on them than yourself? If your primary focus was on helping your customers, your employees, even your boss, more than any expectation of personal gain? You would soon find that what you received in return was far more than what you ever expected, and certainly more than you gave.

When you fully embrace the power of giving to others more than you expect to receive, you begin to receive more—not only of what you expected but also of what you never imagined you could receive.

Follow the principle of becoming a GOMER and watch how you will immediately begin to live a Better Life.

NUMBER FIVE

The fifth answer is a simple formula: ***EMC^2***!

Einstein was onto something, but that's not what this is about. This formula stands for Every Moment Counts! And it's so important it should be repeated *twice*, hence the "squared."

Every Moment Counts!

The popular adage is to live each moment as though it were your last. Well, actually, it is!

This moment, right now as I am speaking to you, will never, *ever*, come again in your life. This day, this hour, this minute, this second is gone forever. And so is this one, and this one, and the next. You see, each moment is indeed your last one of *that* moment. You can't get it back. You can't reproduce it.

No matter what moment you choose, it's always unique, different, and new. When you visit somewhere, say on vacation, you probably try to cram in as much as you can to remember the experience. Even if you return there on vacation sometime in the future, it's not the same. Things have changed, people have changed, places have changed, you have changed, and the moments have changed. So, while the second time may be similar in some ways to the first, it is always different.

We experience our lives one moment at a time, and each moment passes into the next. If you want to truly transform your life, you must learn to make the most out of every moment—yes, even the hard ones. There is power in learning from our challenges, in experiencing both the good and the bad with all that we are. Learning from our mistakes makes our futures brighter, and it gives us power and experience to tackle greater challenges. Truly experiencing joy and happiness in those moments of our lives helps us to remember what life really is all about.

Make the most of your moments and, whenever possible, help others do the same. Sharing moments with others makes our own experiences more powerful. The most beautiful sunset to behold is even more beautiful when we share the experience with someone else.

The value of one second may not seem like much until you ask an Olympic swimmer who just came in second place. The value of one minute may not seem important until you ask the person who just missed their train. The value of one hour, out of all the hours of our days, may not matter until you ask someone who is waiting in a hospital waiting room for their loved one to come out of surgery.

None of us knows how many moments we have or have left. The only certainty is that we each have a finite number of moments.

Don't let fear, anxiety, and worry control your life. There is no point in working so hard to keep fear, anxiety, and worry at bay that you never actually enjoy your life in the process. The time to enjoy it is now. To live a Better Life!

Live your dreams; live your life. Don't simply endure your time or exist day by day. Choose to live! Live every day, cherish every moment, and don't let one more go to waste, no matter how old or young you are.

There you go. Those are the five answers to the question of how you can live a Better Life.

Each day being genuinely grateful for every aspect of your life with **The Responsibility of Gratitude**. Discover your passion and follow your dreams so that you **Leave Your Fingerprints**. Always do the right thing and **Live the HIGH Life** with honor and integrity in all that you do. **Be a GOMER** and give others more than you expect to receive in every area of your life, and be fully present in each moment with **EMC²** by making every moment count!

That's all the time I have.

Thank you very much for listening.

ABOUT THE AUTHOR

Michael Jenet was born in Belgium and moved to the United States when he was seven years old. He is an eight-year veteran of the U.S. Air Force.

An international best-selling and award-winning author, *A Better Life* was first published in 2015 but was later put out of print by the original publisher. Jenet started Journey Institute Press to keep other authors from having the same fate.

Along with his first book, *MOTIVESTIONS*, the 'Better' series includes *A Better Life, A Better Work,* with a third in the series on the way.

He lives in Colorado with his wife and family.

JOURNEY INSTITUTE PRESS

Journey Institute Press is a non-profit publishing house created by authors to flip the publishing model for new authors. Created with intention and purpose to provide the highest quality publishing resources available to authors whose stories might otherwise not be told.

JI Press focusses on women, BIPOC, and LGBTQ+ authors without regard to the genre of their work.

As a Publishing House, our goal is to create a supportive, nurturing, and encouraging environment that puts the author above the publisher in the publishing model.

Guide Point North Publishing is an Imprint of Journey Institute Press, a division of 50 in 52 Journey, Inc.

NOTE: The world of publishing has changed dramatically. This has also affected authors and their ability to let readers know about their books. Today, most people buy books based on word of mouth.

If you would like to help this author, please consider leaving an honest review of this book on retail sites and book community sites.

www.ingramcontent.com/pod-product-compliance
Lightning Source LLC
Chambersburg PA
CBHW042029050526
44107CB00123B/1417/J